A Voice Unheard

A Voice Unheard

The Latimer Case
and People with Disabilities

Ruth Enns

Fernwood Publishing

Electronic versions of this book, in HTML, as well as a limited number of large print photocopies are available to individuals from:
Fernwood Publishing
Box 9409, Stn. A,
Halifax, Nova Scotia,
B3K 5S3
Tel: (902) 422-3302
Fax: (902) 422-3179
fernwood@istar.ca
www.home.istar.ca/~fernwood

Editing: Todd Scarth
Cover image: Alexandra Michaels
Design and production: Beverley Rach
Printed and bound in Canada by: Hignell Printing Limited

A publication of:
Fernwood Publishing
Box 9409, Station A
Halifax, Nova Scotia
B3K 5S3

Fernwood Publishing Company Limited gratefully acknowledges the financial support of the Ministry of Canadian Heritage and the Canada Council for the Arts for our publishing program.

Le Conseil des Arts   The Canada Council
du Canada   for the Arts

Canadian Cataloguing in Publication Data

A voice unheard

Includes bibliographical references.
ISBN 1-55266-014-1

1. Latimer, Robert W. (Robert William) -- Trials, litigation, etc.   2. Latimer, Tracy, 1981-1993.   3. Handicapped -- Canada.   I. Title.

HV1559.C3E55 1999   362.4'0971   C99-950125-9

Contents

Dedication

This book is dedicated to all the Tracy Latimers who must cope with misunderstanding and abuse from those on whom they depend for the necessities of life.

It is also dedicated to parents like my own who do not follow the path Robert Latimer chose. My parents have my admiration and respect for their faith, imagination and perseverance in caring for both me and my late sister, Leona, through the best and worst times.

But most of all this book is dedicated to my husband who chose to join his life with mine. Without his support this book would not have been possible.

Acknowledgements

This book may be credited to one person but it was the result of efforts by many people. The articulation of the disability community's views on disability were facilitated by the support and assistance of the Council of Canadians with Disabilities. I greatly appreciate having being given access to their files and background material, their research assistance and their admirable patience in answering my many questions.

Thank you to the Manitoba League of Persons with Disabilities for their assistance. The Canadian Centre on Disability Studies has also been very helpful in providing research assistance.

Thank you to those disabled people who were willing to relate their personal experiences with disability, putting them in someone else's hands. Such stories have so often been used for purposes not intended by those who shared them. Hopefully this book does justice to their faith in me.

Several readers spent hours critiquing this manuscript; among them: Hedy Martens' counselling and teaching background provided valuable feedback; Doug and Joyce Penner brought their publishing experience to this task; and others. I am also grateful to my siblings for supporting me throughout this project. Several of them read portions of the manuscript from the perspective of their own expertise. Professor Mel Wiebe contributed his knowledge of nineteenth century Britain, Dr. Vicki Strang her nursing perspective and Charles Wiebe his legal background. Ron Wiebe of IOS kept my computer functioning and Dr. Ellen Anderson provided many insightful comments.

Thanks to the people at Fernwood Publishing—Wayne Antony for his help through the whole process and Beverley Rach for designing the layout and cover of the book. Finally, thanks also to Todd Scarth for editing the manuscript, Debbie Mathers for preparing the final text, and Alexandra Micheals for the cover art.

Introduction

The Robert Latimer case has become a flash point in the Canadian debate on assisted suicide and euthanasia. Despite his confession to the crime of killing his disabled daughter, two convictions for second-degree murder and two failed appeals to the Saskatchewan Court of Appeal this farmer from Wilkie, Saskatchewan has become a champion for mercy killing.

By his blatant support for the killing of disabled people unable to speak for themselves, Latimer has served one major purpose. He has brought such murders out from behind closed doors and forced the Canadian public to address an issue most would rather not acknowledge.

However, the daughter he killed remains shrouded in the mists of disability. Little is known about her beyond her physical and mental defects and few have bothered to find out who she was or how she communicated with the people around her. She is not alone in that isolation. Her experiences as well as her treatment in the courts and by the media resonate with the disabled community.

Organizations of disabled citizens have objected to the predominantly negative presentation of Tracy inside and outside the courtroom but their objections have been met with at best patronizing pats on the head and at worst outright hostility. The reasons they oppose lenience for Robert Latimer have not been adequately investigated or understood by their fellow Canadians.

This book is an attempt to present that neglected view, to give voice to those who are consistently unheard. Until they are heard, the discussion on euthanasia and assisted suicide will remain incomplete.

Chapter One

Tracy on Trial

The evening of October 12, 1993 Robert Latimer decided to kill his oldest child, Tracy.[1] It had been less than two weeks since Sue Rodriguez lost her Supreme Court bid for a constitutional exemption in her battle for a physician-aided death. Public support for assisted suicide was high.

Earlier that day Latimer's wife, Laura, had taken Tracy to Saskatoon to see Dr. Anne Dzus, a pediatric orthopaedic surgeon, and was told the operation they had been waiting a year for would not reconstruct Tracy's dislocated right hip, as they had expected; instead it would likely remove the upper part of her femur, or thigh bone, leaving her leg limp.

Tracy had already had three surgeries for complications from her severe spastic cerebral palsy. When Laura gave birth to her, the fetal heart monitor was broken, which prevented the attending staff from detecting Tracy's dangerously slow heart rate. When she later testified for her husband in court, Laura blamed the broken monitor for the lack of timely medical intervention for the baby and Tracy's subsequent cerebral palsy. (More recent research blames cerebral palsy on factors often occurring earlier in the pregnancy.[2])

The medical staff didn't recognize Tracy's seizures until they were frequent and severe enough to require a transfer to Saskatoon's University Hospital. There they were brought under control and she went home. Four months later the seizures recurred worse than before and this time it took the drug Rivotril to bring the number down to a half dozen minor seizures daily. That rate, which the doctors considered non-threatening, remained stable for the rest of her life.

The result of these difficulties was brain damage leaving Tracy with severe spastic cerebral palsy. She would not develop like other children her age and the distorted messages from her brain would pull her growing body out of alignment.

The first two surgeries to deal with that misalignment came when Tracy was four and eight. They stretched some tendons and severed others to make her more symmetrical and head off the hip dislocation common in children like her. After the second she spent some time in a body cast, which caused some problems in caring for her. However, little evidence surfaced that Tracy herself experienced any more discomfort than anyone else in a cast. In fact, for the first time in her life she was able to stand propped against a wall or table. Dr. Dzus later testified in court that this soft tissue surgery was considered successful, although Tracy's spine still curved.

By her third surgery on August 27, 1992 her back had bent and twisted, cramping her internal organs and making eating difficult. The surgery attached stainless steel rods to Tracy's spine to reduce her scoliosis.

Tracy came through the gruelling ordeal with flying colours. After such surgery most children stay in hospital at least one to two weeks but Tracy went home after only six days. Her eating improved and she was free of the respiratory ailments that had plagued her before. In mid-September, just a few days after her two-week follow-up visit to Dr. Dzus, she returned to school.

In November the doctor was still hearing reports of Tracy's improving health. Her right hip seemed destined to go out of joint, although at that point the range of motion was still good and Tracy showed signs of pain only when that range was tested. Further surgery had to be postponed for at least a year to allow Tracy's body to heal completely and lay down enough bone to fuse her spine.

By this time the Latimers had had two other children. Brian was almost three years younger than Tracy, and Lindsay was five years younger. Laura had had a miscarriage two years before Tracy was killed and in late 1992 she became pregnant again. To prevent another miscarriage the Latimers used more respite help than they had before.

The Wilkie group home (which Laura had helped plan) was full, so Tracy was booked into a home in North Battleford. That summer she stayed there four times: twice in June as an experiment, then three months from July 5 to October 3 during the last part of Laura's pregnancy and the adjustment to new baby Lee, and again from October 8 to October 11 when Laura had her tubal ligation. Before that summer, the Latimers had used other respite services frequently.

On October 12, doctors determined that Tracy's hip joint was worse than they had thought, and advanced the surgery date to November 4, less than a month later. They also wanted to admit Tracy a few days early to make sure her nutritional status would let her tolerate the surgery; at this point she was severely underweight. Laura later testified that a short time before Tracy died she weighed forty-four and a half pounds, the most she had ever weighed but in court Laura said both she and Irene Froess from the developmental centre had questioned this at the time. When Tracy was weighed before she went to the group home she had weighed thirty-eight pounds and Laura said she had not gained since then. The last weigh-in occurred shortly after

Tracy on Trial

Tracy got home on October 3, 1993.

Several years earlier the Latimers had refused a gastrostomy, or feeding tube, for Tracy partly on the advice of Robert Latimer's sister, a nurse, who had told them such tubes are just the first step in prolonging the dying process. However, Robert Latimer also had a fear of such devices. He considered vaccinations cruel, and in his youth he had been teased about his squeamishness at facing a dentist. Nevertheless, Dzus said nothing was medically preventing Tracy's surgery.

While Laura and Tracy were in Saskatoon, Kathleen Johnson, a Social Services worker with the Community Living Division in North Battleford, phoned the farm about the application Laura had submitted after the baby's birth to permanently place Tracy in the group home. Robert Latimer answered the phone. He was at home because it was harvest and because he avoided doctor's offices.

A placement meeting had been scheduled for the next day, October 13, but Latimer told Johnson things were not urgent and they didn't want to proceed at that point. Dr. Snyder testified that Social Services assumes responsibility for all such children when they reach adult age and encourages all of them to leave home by the age of eighteen or twenty. Some parents remain involved even after that but some leave all decisions up to this department. According to his confession on November 4 Latimer had no intention of having Tracy institutionalized; he had disagreed with Laura when Johnson discussed the application with them in September.

When Laura got home from Saskatoon she gave her husband the bad news about the change in plans. She said they were both devastated at the thought of Tracy being "mutilate(d)." They disregarded the doctor's assurance that "in the majority of children (the surgery)[3] is successful in decreasing their pain" and instead Laura wished for a Dr. Jack Kevorkian (the U.S. advocate of assisted suicide who was receiving much public attention at that time). In his confession Latimer said he decided that evening to end Tracy's life. According to his confession, after spending a week mulling over the method he would use, he settled on exhaust fumes rather than a gun or drugs.

On Sunday, October 24 he waited for Laura to take the other three children to church at 11 A.M., leaving him to take care of Tracy. While Tracy sat alone in the house in her wheelchair, he ran around the yard for half an hour getting the rags, coat, sleeping bag, hoses and clamps his plan required. Then he returned to the house, picked her up out of her wheelchair, carried her to his blue GMC half-ton truck and drove to the quonset at the north end of the yard.[4]

There he propped her behind the wheel with the rags, coat and sleeping bag, leaving her face uncovered. He connected a hose to the

11

tailpipe and ran it into the cab through the back sliding window, started the motor and closed the door.

For half an hour he sat on a tractor tire in the box of the truck outside the sliding window watching as Tracy jerked several times while the carbon monoxide levels in her blood climbed to 80 percent. He said he timed the whole thing but did not say why. After a while he couldn't see her anymore because the fumes fogged up the windows. In his confession as reported by Corporal Kenneth Lyons, Latimer said, "I thought if she cried I'd pull her out."

Around noon, half an hour after he started the motor, Latimer turned it off. He drove back to the house and carried Tracy's body, limp and reeking of exhaust fumes, back to her bed in the room she shared with her ten-year-old brother, Brian. He arranged her body to make it appear she had died in her sleep and waited for the rest of the family to come home.

They returned at 1:30 p.m. Laura started to get lunch, then fifteen minutes later went to get Tracy and immediately cried out for her husband to phone the hospital. The personnel there told him to call the police as well.

Constable Nick Hartle of the Wilkie RCMP detachment got the dispatch call at 2 p.m. He phoned Latimer who told him Tracy had died in her sleep. Fifteen minutes later Hartle was at the farm. He had called the Biggar Funeral Home—Latimer's choice—and the coroner was also on his way.

On his arrival Hartle found Latimer on the porch. "Bob was quite calm about it," he told the court. He found Laura and the children in Tracy and Brian's room. Laura was breastfeeding baby Lee. "They weren't crying but they were very red-eyed. They had been crying."

The coroner, Dr. Kislen Bhairo, who had been Tracy's doctor from 1981, when she was six months old, to 1990, arrived. While he examined her body for the cause of death Laura watched, holding two-month-old Lee. Latimer walked in and out of the bedroom.

Not finding the causes of death, such as suffocation from vomit or mucous, common in people with severe cerebral palsy, Bhairo and the police decided on an autopsy and Hartle took pictures of Tracy's body. Before he left the house Bhairo ordered the autopsy for the next morning.

At this point Latimer told Hartle he had put Tracy down for a nap around 12:30 p.m. and that she had had some pain and discomfort. He also briefly recounted her medical history. The police officer phoned the Latimers' relatives and friends to assist the family.

Between 2:45 p.m. and 3:45 p.m. the funeral home collected the body and the autopsy papers. Hartle asked Latimer to leave the children for a private talk in Tracy's bedroom. Latimer reiterated his earlier statement that nothing unusual had occurred before Laura and the children left for church, that there had been no evidence of new medical problems. He talked about Tracy's daily pain from her dislocated hip, her recent three-month stay at the North Battleford Children's Group Home, her surgery a year earlier and what the scheduled surgery was supposed to have done.

Hartle said when he informed Latimer there would be an autopsy Latimer "interjected and said, 'I want her cremated.'" According to Hartle, throughout this examination Latimer was "very controlled" and showed no sign of having cried.

Hartle then took Laura aside for a similar discussion. She was more emotional than Latimer had been although she didn't break down. At the end of the session he told her that her husband wanted Tracy cremated. "She seemed quite shocked at it and I noticed that she was visibly taken aback." he testified. However, after Hartle had finished talking to her, Latimer took her into the master bedroom and, when they emerged a few minutes later, Laura consented to the cremation.

Latimer made Hartle some coffee. At one point he became nervous and dropped some old coffee grounds but when the conversation shifted to the farm, he relaxed. He had "just completed the farming," Hartle said. "It was a good year."

When friends began arriving Hartle left. Back at the office he phoned the coroner advising him of his concern about a possible "mercy killing."

The morning of October 27, the day of Tracy's funeral and cremation, Hartle phoned the pathologist, Dr. Ranjit Waghray, to ensure that he had all the necessary samples before it was too late. When Hartle got the results from the Regina crime lab on November 1 he changed the focus of the investigation from sudden death to homicide and scheduled a search warrant for November 4. This was the day Tracy was to have had surgery.

The North Battleford RCMP, assisting the Wilkie detachment, got Latimer out of bed at 8 a.m. and took him to their own headquarters. They informed him several times of his right to consult a lawyer. Each time he refused. At the station he confessed, breaking down during his account of the murder. The officers treated Latimer with empathy while questioning him. Sergeant Robert Conlon offered him food and took him outside to smoke several cigarettes.

Later that day Latimer showed about a dozen police and various experts around the crime scene. They took photos and a video and collected items from the house, the yard, the quonset where Tracy had been killed and from the burning-barrel where Latimer had tried to destroy evidence. One of the police officers there that day was Corporal

A Voice Unheard

Allan Lavallee. He had known Latimer socially for nine years and played on the same ball team. To him Latimer "appeared basically normal" but "under a good deal of stress."

After the walk through—as the police called the search—they took Latimer back to North Battleford where he was formally charged with first-degree murder. Mid-afternoon Laura arrived and asked to see her husband. The police gave them a room where Latimer finally told her what he had done. Later that day he met with two lawyers for the first time.

* * * * *

"This is terrible!" Georgina Heselton said to her husband, Allan, as she read and reread a little article in the Regina *Leader Post* she was holding that November day in 1993.[5] It said a forty-year-old farmer in the Wilkie, Saskatchewan area had been taken into custody by the RCMP and had confessed to killing his disabled daughter, Tracy, with exhaust fumes from his truck. The farmer, Robert Latimer, claimed to have done it out of compassion to end her pain.

The story horrified Heselton and in June 1998, looking back on the previous four and a half years of trials and appeals, she was as convinced as ever that Latimer's behaviour and excuses were inexcusable. "How terrible to kill a child. You just don't do that," she said when I spoke to her.

To her, Tracy's helplessness and the public misinterpretation of the girl's capabilities made her remember her own childhood. Like Tracy Latimer, Heselton had grown up in rural Saskatchewan. Home was a little log cabin six miles north of Churchbridge near the Manitoba border where she lived with her parents, two sisters and a brother.

In 1953 polio left her completely paralyzed. She was thirteen. Tracy Latimer died one month short of her thirteenth birthday. Like Tracy "I couldn't feed myself at first," Heselton said. After a year in hospital where she got little or no physiotherapy, she fought her way back to wellness and, with the help of a doctor in Melville, Saskatchewan she regained enough control of her body to walk with crutches and abandon her wheelchair.

The only lasting effect of her illness was weakness in her hips and right leg. At the time of her complete paralysis no one could have known how self-reliant she would become. Her parents would have wondered when their little girl's suffering would end or if it ever would. At the time, polio was often fatal and there were few services to accommodate survivors' needs. Their futures seemed as bleak as Tracy's did.

However, after Heselton's recovery her parents didn't let the disability and her prolonged absence from home change her status in the family. As the oldest child she had always taken on many responsibilities so she carried on with house and farm chores in addition to school work.

After leaving the hospital, where she had finished grade eight, she used a correspondence course for grade nine because it wasn't offered in the local one-room school. She finished the secondary grades in the second-floor high school in Churchbridge, which had no elevator. She made her own way up and down the stairs. At home she even took on the traditionally male job of driving a tractor, crawling through dirt and grease to repair a tiller wheel that repeatedly fell off. "I was in my glory," she recalled.

Yet, despite her obvious accomplishments, she was stunned one day to hear relatives whispering about her, "She'll never get married. Who will look after her when her parents are gone?" To them her weaker body parts totally eclipsed her strengths and attractive features just as Tracy's personality was hidden behind her abnormalities. In the limited imaginations of their extended family members, both she and Tracy were doomed to a life of isolation and dependency.

Heselton became one of the first Churchbridge graduates to attend university. She got a bachelor's degree in Commerce, an area she thought would give her a good job, and it did. In 1967 she married Allan, a technical engineer, and tried being a stay-at-home housewife for a few months. That drove her "up the walls" so she went back to work. Even giving birth to and caring for two boys didn't keep her from her career.

She eventually reached and stayed at the management levels of the Saskatchewan civil service until post-polio syndrome forced her to retire in 1987. Throughout her career she owned and drove her own car without special controls.

Despite her long marriage and obvious love for her husband she bristles at the assumption of many people that he is a saint for condescending to marry a disabled woman. "There was none of this he-was-looking-after-me business," she said. In fact, she nursed him through a major illness.

However, she realizes she was fortunate. "If Bob Latimer had been my dad I'd have been different," she said. "We don't know that Tracy might have gone on to do all sorts of things."

Although the Latimer case caught her eye early, she didn't know then how much it would encroach on the lives of disabled people across the country. But her alarm bells had gone off and wouldn't be silenced.

A Voice Unheard

* * * *

In November 1993 Pat Danforth, then in Ottawa, was told by a friend about the Latimer case. She too thought, "How terrible," but then put it out of her mind. "Murder is murder. He would be convicted and that would be that."

At the time she didn't foresee the role Latimer would play in the Canadian assisted suicide debate, nor how he would be defended in court a year later.

A decade earlier, disabled Canadians had won their rightful place in the Charter of Rights and Freedoms. It guaranteed them the same protection under the law as able-bodied citizens so it seemed inconceivable that a lawyer would even consider using the victim's disabilities to rationalize murder.

Danforth also didn't know how the media and the public would react or that her own life would take her into the middle of the fray.

* * * * *

About a month after the murder Heselton was in Winnipeg for a meeting of the Council of Canadians with Disabilities (CCD). She was a representative for the Saskatchewan Voice of People with Disabilities, one of eight provincial organizations and several other national groups forming the national umbrella body.

One evening they saw a BBC2 video dated May 2, 1991 on the Nazis' attempts to rid Germany of its disabled people. When it ended she said, "It's still happening. There's a farmer in Wilkie, Saskatchewan who killed his disabled daughter."

It was the first time the case had been brought to the attention of the council. They didn't respond immediately.

* * * * *

On Monday morning, November 7, 1994 Robert William Latimer pleaded not guilty to the charge of first-degree murder. As the Honourable Justice Ross Wimmer later explained while charging the jury, while both first- and second-degree murder involve the intent to kill, first-degree also is premeditated, planned.

Since the onus in criminal cases is on the Crown to prove the guilt of the accused beyond a reasonable doubt, Crown counsel Randy Kirkham's witnesses had to prove, not only that Latimer killed his daughter, but that he planned to kill her. They showed that Tracy had died by carbon monoxide poisoning, that the gas could not have been pro-

16

duced by a faulty furnace or water heater and that only Tracy's father could have killed her.

Corporal Kenneth Lyons, who together with Sergeant Robert Conlon had taken the confession, quoted Latimer's reason for the murder. "(Surgery) was more complicated than what we had expected so we just couldn't see another operation. She'd be confined to a cast for I don't know what the time was so I felt the best thing for her was that she be put out of pain." Dr. Richard Snyder, a cerebral palsy expert who had examined Tracy in 1985, related the services available to families like the Latimers: financial aid, early school placement, the various therapists assisting with everything from feeding and speech to electric wheelchairs and integration into regular schools and the community. He showed that Robert Latimer had many options other than murder.

Mark Brayford was Latimer's second lawyer. His first was Richard Gibbons but by the end of November 1993 Latimer had switched without explanation to Brayford. The interview by CBC TV Saskatoon, which became evidence in both trials, aired only a few weeks after Brayford took over the case. In the interview Robert Latimer was already talking about receiving public support for his actions.

Because cross-examination follows the initial examination of the witness, Brayford presented no witnesses in this trial. Because Kirkham did not re-examine any witnesses the defence consistently had the last word. In cross-examination Brayford merely asked Crown witnesses to corroborate his client's contention that the victim's life had been a helpless, hopeless existence, that Tracy's constant "torture" was increasing, that Latimer was an honest man and a wonderful father and that Tracy's death had been painless. He argued the murder was necessary to prevent the even greater injustice of letting her live in constant pain.

After consulting with Brayford, Kirkham decided not to call six of his fifteen witnesses who were not essential to his case. The prosecutor had listed Laura Latimer as his witness but, when it was her turn to take the stand, he said he wanted to spare her and her testimony wasn't necessary. However, Brayford successfully persuaded the court to allow cross-examination even if Kirkham chose not to question her. Her testimony was crucial to his argument. Kirkham asked her only one question, whether she had had any dreams for Tracy to which Laura replied that she had wanted the best possible life for her daughter. Brayford then had her recount Tracy's life in terms of the pain she experienced, contrasting her later pain and suffering with her early happy years.

Kirkham did not directly challenge much of the defence's case except to point out Latimer's other options. In his closing remarks to the jury he pointed out that Latimer had initially lied to the police about how and when Tracy had died. He also related several of Tracy's enjoyments but during his examination of the witnesses he did not refute the constant pain theory or give a different view of her life. Brayford used his last word to solidify the Latimers' version in the minds of the jurors before they retired to consider their verdict. Because Brayford's points went uncontested during witness testimonies, they became prima facie evidence that Tracy's life was indeed as bleak and painful as the Latimers claimed. Prima facie evidence is unproven evidence treated as fact because it is not disputed.

On November 15 closing arguments were heard. In his charge to the jury the next day Justice Wimmer rejected the Crown's argument of cold-blooded murder, conceding that Latimer probably acted out of compassion. However, he did not allow the defence of necessity or suicide either.

In this case necessity was the closest the defence could get to a plea of mercy killing. Canadian criminal law does not allow mercy killing, or compassionate homicide as some would call it. Necessity is significantly different from mercy killing. The latter involves killing someone to avoid suffering, however suffering is defined. Necessity as defined by Wimmer meant there were no options other than a fate worse than the one for which the person is on trial. He gave the example of someone facing criminal charges for break-and-enter when the accused had broken into an empty cabin to avoid freezing to death. Self defence would be another example. Wimmer did not allow the necessity plea because Latimer had other viable options.

The jury, after repeatedly asking for clarification on the difference between first- and second-degree murder charges, pronounced him not guilty of first-degree but guilty of second-degree murder which allows for parole after ten years instead of twenty-five. Latimer, in his only statement in court said the jury was "not human." His lawyer appealed the decision.

* * * * *

Catherine Lambeth first heard about Robert Latimer on her car radio as she drove through Winnipeg to her mother's house. The story caught her attention because her oldest daughter has cerebral palsy and, at the time, Samantha was about Tracy's age.

Lambeth's legal credentials and marriage to lawyer Grant Mitchell also made her sensitive to the arguments defending Latimer's actions. She told me that both she and her husband felt the defence line of reasoning about Tracy was an insult to their profession and to their role as parents.

Tracy on Trial

Lambeth wrote letters to radio and television shows and to newspapers. When she and Mitchell began to fear that Latimer's legal team might seek an executive pardon, they wrote to the federal minister of justice advising against it. Mitchell spoke out in public. In his December 9, 1994 address to the human rights conference of the Canadian Legal Education Association he expressed his disappointment that no organization representing disabled people had spoken out against this murder.

Theresa Ducharme of Winnipeg had intervened in cases of assisted deaths across the country. She had gone to Montreal to talk Nancy B. into continuing her life and, with the help of a lawyer from Grant Mitchell's firm, had opposed Sue Rodriguez' appeal to the Supreme Court. She had also collected over 20,000 names on a petition supporting her opposition to Rodriguez' appeal. When she heard of the Latimer case, she immediately took up the cause again. To her these cases were all the same in devaluing human lives touched by disability.

Ducharme tried to convince the Manitoba League of Persons with Disabilities and CCD to join her efforts. She heads a small Winnipeg-based organization, People in Equal Participation (PEP), which claims about 150 members. Ducharme is the only spokesperson the tiny group has had in the two decades since its inception.

PEP meets around cultural and religious accessibility issues. As such its goals didn't fall within the mandate of either the provincial or national advocacy groups, neither of which were affiliated with hers. Although they agreed with her opposition to Latimer, they had other views on assisted suicide. They also couldn't respond as quickly as she could. As a much larger organization representing several hundred thousand disabled people across the country, CCD's spokespeople had to go through the lengthy process of consulting their membership before they could step in front of any microphones.

So Ducharme filled the temporary void. When she heard Mitchell address the conference she wheeled up to him and challenged him to support his brave words with action. Before he took up the gauntlet, he polled the more than fifty lawyers in his firm and found that about 20 percent supported his idea of offering legal services to PEP.

Six weeks after Mitchell encountered Ducharme, CCD passed a resolution at its January 21–22, 1995 meeting denouncing "the deliberate taking of a disabled person's life without their express consent."[6] To them "such actions are properly defined as murder in the Criminal Code of Canada." Their position maintained that murders such as that of Tracy Latimer have to be treated just like the murder of any other person.

However, where PEP remained focussed on the case, CCD took a broader approach. It launched a public awareness campaign including several public vigils in memory of Tracy and other disabled victims murdered by their care-givers. They began publishing and circulating the *Latimer Watch*, a newsletter devoted to the Latimer case, euthanasia and related issues. They protested government cutbacks jeopardizing essential services and any action denying disabled people equal constitutional rights. They opposed the Senate Committee on Euthanasia and Assisted Suicide recommendations which proposed lenient sentencing in murders claiming compassionate motives because of the victims' disabilities. And they reaffirmed their commitment to promoting a positive image of disabled people as contributing members of society.

* * * * *

While CCD was establishing its position on Latimer it was still dealing with the debate over Sue Rodriguez' request for a physician-assisted suicide and was reluctant to get involved in the murder case.

Its member group in British Columbia, Rodriguez' home province, was very influenced by her struggle and had intervened on her behalf in her Supreme Court appeal. In fact, they had taken the debate farther than she had, advocating the omission of a terminal illness safeguard. They proposed including anyone wanting to commit suicide but unable to do so unassisted. Rodriguez had asked only for a personal exemption to the law against assisted suicide. She wanted simply a device she could control herself with a doctor supplying the drugs.

CCD[7] had also intervened in Rodriguez' favour but with much trepidation. They feared the hasty debate forced by her rapid physical degeneration would not allow adequate consideration of safeguards for the majority of disabled people, the ones who value their lives and want to keep living. Consequently CCD urged the court to put a two-year moratorium on any action beyond this individual exemption to allow for full public debate. Their support also hinged on foolproof safeguards to protect vulnerable citizens from potential abuses.

CCD, the BC group, some members in the Saskatchewan Voice and Confederation des Organismes de Personnes Handicapees du Quebec (COPHAN) saw legalized assisted suicide as part of the self-determination for which they had been struggling since the beginning of their self-advocacy movement. To them, people too disabled to commit suicide unassisted should have the same right to end their lives as able-bodied people. Denying them such a final wish would be prejudice.

However, CCD understood as well as PEP that disabled people's lives are already perceived as not worth living. Both groups were afraid legalizing assisted suicide would increase pressure from medical professionals and others to end their lives, freeing medical resources for others.

The fear evident in both their presentations had grown out of first-hand experience. They were keenly aware of the widespread ignorance about disability at all levels of Canadian society. Not even all medical professionals nor all disabled people themselves were aware of the goals and achievements of their advocacy organizations nor of the issues facing many in their ranks.

While PEP based its opposition primarily on the sanctity of all human life, CCD feared the potentially deadly consequences of mixing misperceptions with assisted suicide. Disabled people were already in much greater danger of being abused than able-bodied people.

By June 1996 the Latimer case had forced CCD to concede the inadequacy of any conceivable safeguards and reverse its stand on assisted suicide. Jim Derksen, former chair of CCD and a member of the counsel's national human rights committee said disabled people don't really need any more help in ending their lives; they already have easy access to assisted death. When able-bodied people become suicidal their behaviour is generally seen as aberrant, something with underlying causes crying out for compassion and healing. However, when disabled people become suicidal our society is too quick to withdraw that lifeline and actually help carry out the very behaviour deemed abnormal in the rest of the population.

So disabled opponents of legalized assisted suicide were willing to forego self-determination at the end of their lives to ward off a much greater evil. They wanted assurance of the right to live before they would even consider fighting for the right to die.

However, some disabled people were as swayed by defence and media rhetoric as the general population was. The BC group went so far as to form a right-to-die committee, although they supported CCD's position on Latimer. A minority of Saskatchewan Voice members supporting Latimer left the organization but the remaining majority unified in their opposition to assisted suicide because of the Latimer murder case.

Regardless of how much this split slowed down CCD's participation in the Latimer case or how divided the organization appeared to outsiders or how much the schism may have confused the debate, CCD still sees their internal process of decision-making as positive. Mel Graham, CCD's information officer in the Winnipeg head office, says member groups' freedom to work out their own positions in such instances is vital to the learning process. "You have to review all the time."

Nevertheless, one result of their lengthy decision making and reversal was that events raced ahead of the disabled community's responses and the lag allowed public misconceptions of and support for Latimer to build. Consequently the disabled organizations were put on the defensive and their position weakened.

Regardless of the side advocates chose in their internal discussion, they all thought the Charter already gave them what they needed, namely the rights of full citizenship including full protection under the law. None of them knew how quickly the discussion would slide from Kevorkian, Rodriguez and assisted suicide to voluntary, then involuntary euthanasia and "mercy killing," nor how willingly the public would confuse assisted suicide with murder just because the victim was disabled and unable to speak. They did not realize at the time that their citizenship rights could be wiped out with the stroke of one judge's pen.

* * * * *

The warm blanket of sympathy surrounding Latimer inside the courtroom, in the media and on the street horrified disabled people. Many of them were in situations similar to Tracy's and they were keenly aware of their own vulnerability. The defence's assertion in court that acquitting Latimer would not be an invitation to euthanasia did not reassure them.

The killing of a disabled child did not come as a shock to most disabled people. Many have experienced abuse themselves. Dick Sobsey of the University of Alberta's Abuse and Disability Project wrote, "Children with disabilities are much more likely to be abused than other children. They are twice as likely to be physically abused and almost twice as likely to be sexually abused."[8] Usually the abusers receive a light sentence or none at all.

Pat Danforth, now back in Regina, urged the Saskatchewan Voice to get involved. She volunteered to become their spokesperson in this case, a role for which she was well suited. She had been the education and equity advisor for the Saskatchewan Human Rights Commission since 1985.

In Winnipeg PEP, with Grant Mitchell's help, applied for and got intervenor status in Latimer's appeal. CCD and the Saskatchewan Voice soon followed suit.

On February 24, 1995 the three judges in the Saskatchewan Court of Appeal heard the submissions and denied the appeal. Opinion on the sentence was spilt. Chief Justice Edward D. Bayda thought it was excessive, cruel and unusual. Latimer's counsel launched an appeal to the Supreme Court on the grounds that Latimer's confession should not have been admitted as evidence. The appeal also raised the charges laid against crown prosecutor Kirkham in June 1996 for obstructing justice through jury tampering. According to a *Globe and Mail* report in

Tracy on Trial

October 1995, Kirkham had asked RCMP officers to "find out the beliefs of prospective jurors on such issues as religion, abortion and mercy killing."[9] Because several of those subjected to the questioning ended up on the jury, the situation might have left the impression that the jury was not impartial. In February 1997 the court found the confession admissible but ordered a new trial because of the prosecutor's actions.

* * * * *

Three years almost to the day after the first trial, the second one began, running from October 27 to November 5, 1997. The verdict came on November 13 and sentencing December 1. Because the previous jury had convicted Latimer of second-degree murder, the charge this time was second- and not first-degree murder.

Defence counsel Mark Brayford concentrated on pain in his opening statement and decreed that, although the pain and the disability both resulted from cerebral palsy, he was not talking about disability.

The Crown attorney, Eric Neufeld, did not ignore the defence line of reasoning as completely as his predecessor had but he, too, ran through the same evidence establishing the defendant's guilt, even though that was not the main issue. Latimer was not denying that he had killed Tracy; he was claiming that her circumstances had given him no other options.

Some of the evidence was a simple rerun of the last trial; because she was unable to attend, Dr. Dzus' testimony from the first trial was read in as evidence. The Crown's witness Dr. David Kemp, the Latimers' family physician who had considerable experience with cerebral palsy, said the last time he saw Tracy was December 1992, ten months before she died. He had treated her before her back surgery for a number of ailments caused by the scoliosis, none of which had recurred afterwards. He said the surgery Tracy was expecting—arthroplasty—is also commonly done for people with severe osteoarthritis.

He told as well about Tracy's frequent hospitalizations for respite before the Wilkie group home was built. Respite programs give caregivers relief either by bringing help into the home or by placing the disabled person in other facilities for short periods, ranging from several hours or overnight to as long as several months.

Brayford's cross-examination focussed on the alleged degenerative nature of cerebral palsy—cerebral palsy is not classified medically as degenerative—and the hopelessness of relieving Tracy's pain with surgery. He asked whether the operation scheduled for November 4, 1993 would have ended Tracy's pain, whether it would have been the last surgery necessary. Of course, the answer was no. The defence described the surgery as detaching her leg from her body, leaving it connected only by muscle, and emphasized how "floppy" it would have been.

Brayford asked about Tracy's pain before the 1992 back surgery and had Dr. Kemp stand up to demonstrate what Tracy's body had looked like before that surgery. He did not ask for a contrasting "after" demonstration but showed pictures of the rods inserted into Tracy's back.

Theresa Huyghebaert, who ran the North Battleford group home where Tracy spent her last summer, said the girl had been there four times between the beginning of June to October 11. Huyghebaert said Tracy's pain was not constant. The pain she did have was relieved by repositioning. She also said Tracy showed pleasure and recognition by smiling. For several weeks in September 1993 she had attended a local school.

Brayford's questions stressed that with Tracy's mental deficiencies she would not ever have learned to read, that school was just entertainment for her. He also pointed out how much work her care required.

Despite the defence's declaration that the trial was not about disability, Brayford asked if Tracy would ever have been able to speak, grow "out of diapers" or be able to "feed herself." He did not link these to pain and suffering. Nor did the Crown challenge this contradiction.

The defence called four witnesses. Two of them, Latimer's sisters, testified to their brother's caring personality, his long-suffering nature, his good parenting skills and his fear of medical devices such as needles and tubes. One of them, a nurse, said she couldn't talk about her work while he was around and during one visit she had noticed him turn over a magazine with a picture of a syringe on the cover to avoid looking at it. Latimer thought vaccinations are cruel. He did not visit Tracy when she was in intensive care after her back surgery. Even intravenous needles were too much for him.

During his recent nine-and-a-half-hour examination of the defendant, the forensic psychiatrist, Dr. Robin Menzies, had found Latimer to be a stubborn man with a phobia about medical interventions causing tissue damage. Despite Latimer's confession and his fear of the very type of medical intervention Tracy had been facing, Menzies said the phobia was not relevant to the murder because it had not prevented him from functioning normally or from participating in Tracy's care. In his opinion Latimer was sane. Brayford's later summary of this testimony said Latimer is "not insane, he's not mentally ill, he's not a psychopath.... he is a loving father that carefully considered his options, a little bit phobic about the medical profession."

When Brayford called Laura Latimer, he again had her recount all the horrors of Tracy's life, showing how her suffering had grown with each surgery. When he got to the 1992 back surgery he emphasized that, although it had had great health benefits, the pain "just seemed to build."

A significant difference between the two trials came when prosecutor Neufeld pointed out weaknesses in the testimonies of Brayford's witnesses. He highlighted several discrepancies in Laura's testimony, especially concerning pain and Tracy's abilities and awareness. He had Laura read her own note to the development centre rhapsodizing about Tracy's improvement since the surgery. He also had her read forty entries in the communications books that travelled with Tracy on her daily school bus trips to and from the centre.

The entries started before the back surgery and continued until October 19, five days before she was killed. The only gap in the books occurred when Tracy was in the group home from July 5 to October 3. All the forty entries told about Tracy's good days—eating and sleeping well and participating in normal childhood activities.

Brayford replied with three entries that mentioned pain, implying that he could produce more if he chose. All three entries were from October 1993 and none was the final entry which had been used by the prosecution as evidence of Tracy's good days.

Dr. Anne Dzus' previous testimony under Brayford's cross-examination had raised the issue of life expectancy. She cited a study that gave ten years as the median life span for children like Tracy—half died before the age of ten, half after. However, when Neufeld asked Dr. David Kemp to comment on life expectancy, the Latimers' family physician acknowledged that children like Tracy have a shorter life expectancy than "fit individuals" but he also said, "Some people live to middle age or older, with good care.... I looked after a lady with cerebral palsy in Wilkie that died in her mid-forties."

The verdict in the second trial was the same as in the first—guilty of second-degree murder—but the sentencing differed. The jury asked Justice Ted Noble whether they could influence the length of the sentence but, as the law requires, that request was denied. They found Latimer guilty as charged but nevertheless recommended that he be given parole eligibility after only one year, not the ten required by law.

Justice Noble deliberated until December 1, 1997 when he gave Latimer a constitutional exemption based on Section 12 of the Charter which guarantees the right not to be subject to cruel or unusual punishment. He sentenced Latimer to only two years with one of them to be served on his own farm.

The Crown appealed the sentence while the defence appealed the verdict. Six disability-rights organizations applied for and got intervenor status. On October 19, 1998 the higher provincial court again heard and denied Latimer's appeal, upholding the ten-year minimum sentence.

* * * * *

When Pat Danforth heard Justice Noble announce the constitutional exemption she couldn't help herself. She broke down and wept. So did several of the other disabled people monitoring the trial inside and outside the courtroom. Other disabled observers reacted with anger. If the facts could clearly establish the guilt of a murderer but the victim's disabilities could cloud the judgement of the media, the public and those representing the law, where could disabled people turn for protection and justice?

Their anger and fear were justified. A closer examination of the testimonies shows that almost everyone involved in both trials was convinced before the proceedings reached the courtroom that death was preferable to Tracy's life. Such an examination reveals discrepancies, omissions and a serious distortion of justice to accommodate this one man.

The Investigation

There was a supportive atmosphere around the suspect that was evident from the beginning, even in the police investigation. While the officers followed the letter of the law in charging Latimer with first-degree murder, they admitted they sympathized with him and treated him with great "empathy."

As soon as Constable Hartle, the first officer on the scene, suspected this was not a natural death, but before he had any evidence of compassionate motives other than Tracy's deformities and an account of her pain from the suspect, he called it a possible "mercy killing."

In court, the two officers who took Latimer's confession both mentioned police sympathy for the man they were arresting. Sergeant Robert Conlon said the police empathized with Latimer. He did not mention Latimer's initial lies although Kirkham pointed them out in his final statement to the jury. Corporal Kenneth Lyons confirmed the sympathy toward Latimer at the police station. When Latimer was being questioned and before he confessed to anything, Lyons repeatedly handed him his motive: "'This is something that you felt you had to do out of love for your daughter, isn't it, Bob?'"

And defence lawyer Brayford later capitalized on that "cordial" atmosphere, portraying his client as open and cooperative. Here the circular logic implied that Latimer's openness after he was found out proved his honesty which, therefore, supported his claim that he acted out of compassion.

The officers' testimonies suggested that they treated him less harshly simply because they saw him as the over-burdened care-giver faced with an unenviable decision. Their primary evidence was the victim's degree of disability and the defendant's account of her situation.

The First Trial Atmosphere

The atmosphere in the courtroom was also sympathetic to the defendant. The trial was a strange game with each side ignoring the other's hypothesis.

Crown counsel Randy Kirkham used RCMP and forensic evidence to point to the guilt of the defendant, the deliberate premeditation of the killing and Latimer's options, placing Tracy's death within the definition of first-degree murder. Latimer's confession, obtained legally and accepted as evidence, said he planned the murder almost two weeks in advance so this should have been an open-and-shut case. Consequently the Crown's plan was simply to get a conviction, not to fully address the defence strategy.

However, it is the prosecutor's role, not merely to prove the crime according to the letter of the law, but also to defeat the opposing side's arguments.

On the other side of the legal game, Latimer's confession, obtained after he refused several times the help of a lawyer, and the admission of premeditation left defence counsel with few options. Brayford could have his client plead guilty and spend a minimum of twenty-five years in jail before parole eligibility or he could challenge the charge by pleading necessity. Latimer could not take the easy way out, the one branding him an over-burdened care-giver. He and his wife, Laura, had been offered too many options, such as permanently placing Tracy in the group home, and he had taken too much care in planning Tracy's death.

For the necessity defence to work Brayford had to show that Latimer had no choice but to kill Tracy, that to refrain from it would have put her in even greater jeopardy. To prove this, he would have to put Tracy's body on trial to divert attention from the guilt of her murderer. This was the strategy he would use.

Kirkham used hard facts while the defence relied heavily on emotional appeal. As a result the prosecutor looked cold and technocratic and his arguments seemed irrelevant, while Brayford came across as warm and caring. Because Kirkham refuted necessity by showing Latimer's options but not by disputing the defence claims of Tracy's deterioration and constant pain, these claims became prima facie evidence. Kirkham only became more heated in his closing statement to the jury, pointing out some of the fallacies in the defence position. Had the prosecutor done its homework to find evidence to contradict the claims about Tracy's pain, in part through consulting the disabled community about pain and common attitudes about disability, Kirkham might have been more effective in the courtroom.

In the defence strategy, evidence of Latimer's guilt was irrelevant. Brayford was not trying to establish his client's innocence. He was trying to prove Latimer had no option but to do what he did. He was using the presumed motive of compassion to prove the necessity of the killing and therefore to argue that his client should be exonerated despite his guilt.

During the discussion on Kirkham's decision not to call Laura as a witness Brayford had fought to retain the right to have the last word. That was the reason he had not listed Laura as a witness for the defence. As a result Laura's gloomy portrait of Tracy's life as directed by the defence was the last thing the jury heard before the judge's instructions sent them to consider their verdict.

Prosecution of the crime was damaged even more after the trial when Kirkham was charged with irregularities in jury selection. Although he was acquitted in June 1998, the accusations accentuated the image of Latimer as a victim of injustice.

The Second Trial

In the presentation of the facts, the second trial was a rerun of the first. The atmosphere, however, was slightly different. In this one the Crown attorney, Eric Neufeld, presented more than facts about the murder itself. He also tried to overturn the defence's claims about constant pain, Tracy's lack of awareness or her ability to interact with others. He had Laura acknowledge the benefits of the back surgery and the fact that Tracy had lost weight at home on other occasions. He discredited one of Latimer's sisters by forcing her to admit that she had visited her brother's family only once during the last year of Tracy's life. He also forced Latimer's nurse sister to admit that many people live with feeding tubes for many years. However, he did not challenge the central premise of the defense, that in the right circumstances it might actually be necessary to kill a dependent child.

Brayford repeated his argument of necessity with some new caution. His opening remarks showed a greater awareness of the need to differentiate between pain, suffering and disability. However, he also ludicrously declared that the only common element between Tracy's disability and her pain was the common cause of cerebral palsy. Perhaps he thought that making that distinction allowed him to continue with the necessity defence without appearing to target disabled people, but he didn't elaborate on how he came to such a conclusion. Nor did Neufeld challenge him on that point.

Tracy's pain was caused by her disability which was caused by cerebral palsy. They could not be separated. Pain is a symptom, the body's plea for help. It is a plea the medical profession is designed to answer and was about to for Tracy. But the defence argued that Tracy's pain could be answered only with death.

The Second Sentence

In defending the unprecedented sentence of two years with only one to be served in jail, Justice Ted Noble wrote that he considered, among other things, the difference in evidence between the two trials. He rejected the first prosecutor's accusations that this murder had been committed because Tracy was disabled.

Noble said only the pain was relevant but he himself kept describing Tracy in terms of her disability as much as her pain. He said she was "born with a very severe form of cerebral palsy which left her permanently incapacitated and in order to sustain her life she required constant ongoing total care." Later he wrote that she was Latimer's "tragically debilitated daughter" and that "her health was slowly but steadily deteriorating." These descriptions emphasize dependency or disability, the burden of caring for her and the presumption that she was terminally ill. So, while he said the disabilities had to be separated from the pain, he himself did not do so. To Justice Noble, apparently pain, disability and terminal illness were indistinguishable from each other.

His apparent misunderstanding of disability surfaced again when he cited other instances of mercy killing and compared Tracy with five victims of such homicides. All had been terminally ill adults and the convicted killers received mere slaps on the wrist. Noble described one incident of a nurse administering "a lethal dose of potassium chloride to a comatose patient to shorten his agony." If the patient was truly comatose, was he really in agony? This was the same assumption Brayford had made in his statement to the *Star Phoenix* on November 24, 1993 when he said Tracy was "literally in a vegetative state and was undergoing tremendous pain." People in a vegetative state show no sign of feeling pain.

Justice Noble accepted the defence contention that the murder had been motivated by the victim's pain, ignoring Latimer's confession, which said the motive had been to avoid the surgery by putting her out of pain. The judge overlooked all the evidence contradicting the constant pain theory. He claimed prima facie evidence supported his conclusion that this murder was less culpable than other murders; that is, he said the evidence was "clear and uncontradicted" that this was "that rare act of homicide that was committed for caring and altruistic reasons. That is why, for want of a better term, this is called compassionate homicide."

In Canadian law mercy killing is murder and all those who commit murder, whether motivated by compassion or hatred, fall under the same minimum sentencing laws. The most notable allowance made for motive is whether the deed was premeditated or whether death was the intended result. And justly so. The motive does not alter the fact that the victim is dead and cannot validate the murderer's claim of compassion.

In effect Noble was creating a new category of homicide by using the Charter to circumvent Canadian criminal and minimum sentencing laws. With that he put compassionate homicide on the fast track, bypassing the need for Parliament to pass new laws. He used Section 12 of the Charter to over-ride Section 15 which guarantees disabled people equal protection under the law. Section 12 says, "everyone has the right not to be subjected to any cruel or unusual punishment." Section 15 (1) says, "Every individual is equal before and under the law and has the right to the equal protection and equal benefit of the law without discrimination and, in particular, without discrimination based on race, national or ethnic origin, colour, religion, sex, age or mental or physical disability."

Justice Noble's last justification for lenience in sentencing was public opinion. He used reactions to Latimer's first trial to measure the effects the minimum sentence would have on "standards of decency" as defined by the Supreme Court. But he failed to consider how those reactions had been shaped, how people had heard about the case and what they had heard. He did not consider that the material on which Canadians based those opinions had been filtered through, what I will argue was, a biased media.

Pain, Suffering, Mutilation and Disability

While the defence's stated intention was to reveal Tracy's unending suffering and, therefore, the necessity of killing her, the argument did not stop with pain. It also included suffering, mutilation and disability, and therefore makes sense only if disability is equated with suffering, even without pain. In fact, much of Latimer's defence rested on this common conflation of pain with suffering, mutilation and disability. Without this tangle of terms his repeated references to diapering, recognition and learning ability are inconsistent with the necessity defence.

Laura also confused the terms. Her first thought on hearing the nature of the upcoming surgery was not the pain but, "they were going to start mutilating our little girl." Mutilation is not pain, but disfiguring or disabling. There would certainly have been pain after the surgery but every surgery brings pain, and indications were that the long-term effect of this so-called mutilation would have been less pain, not more.

All of these terms—pain, suffering, mutilation, disability—are highly subjective. In fact, organizations of disabled people rely on self-analysis to determine disability: a person decides for herself whether a given condition prevents her from interacting with her environment.

The medical profession recognizes different pain thresholds, understanding that pain is perceived differently by different people. Prosecutor Neufeld pointed this out in the second trial. Pain is a symptom, not a terminal illness. It should be a signal to look for and treat its cause. Failing that, pain management should be the next option, not a death sentence, and neither Crown prosecutor adequately explored the analgesic alternatives available to Tracy. The autopsy revealed that Tylenol, the only pain relief she was allowed when she was not in hospital, was not present in her body at the time of death; Laura claimed it wasn't effective. It would have been instructive to know how other children like Tracy deal with pain.

Suffering is predominantly a matter of perception; it may involve pain or it may be only a perception of burden resulting from an unwillingness to cope with a disagreeable situation. It has also become a meaningless term, applied to everything from the agony of a painful terminal illness to ordinary male-pattern baldness or a sports team's winless streak. Even Robert Latimer's struggle against due process of law has been labeled suffering.

What is mutilation to some is just the necessary consequences of life-saving or pain-reducing surgery to others. No one describes Terry Fox as mutilated even though he lost, not just a part of a bone, but his whole leg in an attempt to cure his cancer. Yet Tracy's upcoming surgery for a non-life-threatening condition was called mutilation because it wouldn't cure her cerebral palsy.

Despite the inherently subjective nature of these terms Brayford treated them as empirical concepts to be interpreted by able-bodied "experts." He asked doctors and Tracy's mother to assess her degree of pain and discomfort. Neither he nor either of the Crown attorneys consulted disabled people themselves for their truly expert opinion on the suffering involved in living with a disability like cerebral palsy.

On cross-examining Dr. Bhairo, Brayford strayed from Tracy's twisted spine and its effect on her internal organs to her ability to recognize people and her dependency: "was there any suggestion given to you that she could in any way recognize you?" Neither he nor the Crown even attempted to ascertain how this was evidence of pain, suffering or mutilation. Besides, Laura later testified Tracy could recognize immediate family members and in the second trial Dr. Kemp said her vision was impaired.

Brayford asked Bhairo about Tracy's bodily functions concluding, "I take it she was totally dependent upon others." He emphasized that she had to be spoon-fed, diapered and repositioned but did not relate these to pain or suffering either.

In cross-examining Dr. Dzus, Brayford focussed on whether the cerebral palsy would ever have been cured, whether she would ever have been able to sit, eat, do anything unassisted and whether her quality of life had improved during her last year of life. He asked whether the proposed surgery would have cured Tracy's pain for the future but Kirkham did not point out that no surgery comes with a guarantee of complete success, and nobody can expect a life completely free of pain.

Sitting, eating and doing things unassisted have nothing to do with pain, but dwelling on them worked to dehumanize Tracy, to show that, if her brain was so damaged she could not even recognize people, then she herself was not a person and could never have been anything but a burden. In short, that death was preferable to her life. Implicitly she was rendered sub-human and the murder something less than murder. This presumption went unchallenged by the Crown.

In his first trial cross-examination of Dr. Robert Snyder, a developmental pediatrician at the Kinsmen Children's Centre in Saskatoon, Brayford asked whether surgery would have made her hips or back "normal" again. He did not establish what normal means or how it related to Tracy's supposed suffering. According to Laura Latimer's written statements, Tracy's last surgery had alleviated more suffering than it caused, but in the defence argument any pain, even that intended to alleviate more serious pain, was a valid reason to kill her. The Crown's silence in the face of such misinformation is inexcusable. Such reasoning exemplifies some of the most daunting obstacles disabled people face—assumptions and ignorance. Neither has a place in a court of law based on facts, expert opinion and interpretation based on those facts and opinions.

The defence's case was summarized in Laura's emotional statement that her daughter's birth was much more tragic than her death. It was based, not on the testimony of disabled people, the only ones with first-hand experience, but on the unproven notion that, because the disabling event is tragic, a disabled person's entire life is an ongoing tragedy filled with suffering, and is therefore worthless.

The majority of disabled people know otherwise. They value their lives as much as everyone else and they live fulfilled, satisfying lives, even with conditions that are truly degenerative. Only a minority choose death over life but the same is true of the able-bodied population.

By definition permanent disability is incurable so the emphasis on Tracy's unlikely independence was a comment on her disabilities, not on her suffering. All those with a noticeable disability have to put up with these misconceptions daily, and know that they can never measure up as cured or normal. All can imagine a fate like Tracy's.

Feeding Tubes

In contrast Brayford referred to tube feeding as "force feeding." Dr. Anne Dzus immediately responded that the term could have other connotations, but the phrase and his other questions revealed the purpose of his inquiries. The word "force" implies that a gastrostomy would have imposed food on Tracy, that her eating difficulty was her way of refusing food, that she wanted to be starved to death. It implicitly substantiated the suicide defence.

Medical circles have been debating the ethics of gastrostomies. Many see them as Latimer's nurse sister did, as the first step in prolonging life that no longer has any quality. However, many disabled people see this procedure as no more grotesque or unnatural than colostomies which also interrupt the gastro-intestinal tract, for elimination rather than ingestion. Both sustain life. Many disabled children and adults live successfully and happily with gastrostomies just as many live for decades with colostomies. They are not the "pretty unusual stuff" Latimer would have Canadians believe they are. No one bothered to ask whether this interpretation was based on patient reports or on Latimer's fear of medical intervention, particularly anything intruding into the human body such as ordinary needles and tubes.

Constant Pain?

Without the conflation of pain with suffering, mutilation and disability, the defence's case was weak.

Laura's note to the development centre on September 5, 1992, three days after Tracy got home from the back surgery, completely contradicted the allegations of constant intense pain. Laura wrote, "Tracy is doing so well you wouldn't believe it." Twelve days later this same little girl happily took the three-quarter-hour school bus trip back to the centre.

Brayford maintained that, "With greatest deference to all fathers … no one can know what's going on in an infant's mind as well as the child's mother," arguing that Laura's opinion of Tracy's pain level should be the final word on the matter. Disabled people know from experience how wrong that assumption is. While many parents of disabled children, like Georgina Heselton's, treat them no differently than their able-bodied children, some cannot get beyond their grief and disappointment at having an imperfect child. These parents often impose their own perception of the child's suffering onto the youngster, thereby increasing the child's burden.

Prosecutor Neufeld didn't dispute Laura's expertise although he did turn it to the Crown's advantage by asking Laura to read thirty-nine[9] entries in the communications book, starting before her back surgery and ending a week after Robert Latimer decided to kill Tracy, just five days before he carried out his plan. All of these notes were about Tracy's good times: eating, sleeping, participating in school and family activities, playing, making choices and being a little mischievous. The implications of these entries apparently had little influence on the judge, jury and many able-bodied observers. The prosecution didn't spell out the implications.

The three entries put forward by the defence talked about pain and eating problems but even they did not mention constant suffering. Nor did they cover the entire last year as the forty entries had. The first was dated October 13, the day after the long ride to and from Dr. Dzus' office in Saskatoon. The other two were October 16 and 17, 1993. If there were more entries substantiating the defence of unremitting pain, Brayford could have had Laura read them.

Laura's courtroom account said after the 1992 back surgery Tracy was perpetually "miserable," "in a lot of pain," that she had lost interest in eating and couldn't sleep because of the pain. However, her written account did not support the claim that the pain and suffering were unrelenting "torture." It talked about Tracy sleeping, eating, happily participating in family activities and at the centre.

In court Laura contradicted her written assessments of the back surgery by saying, "Tracy was never the same again, never, she was never the happy little girl she used to be, ever again.... She used to be a happy little girl, and she'd turned into someone who just sat slumped, just waiting to be moved." She said Tracy couldn't be rocked anymore after the surgery, that she was in a lot of pain. "Tracy was miserable."

While Laura did admit that Tracy no longer had the same trouble with colds or bronchitis after the back surgery, she didn't explain how Tracy could slump with rods straightening her spine. And Therese Huyghebaert from the North Battleford group home said staff saw Latimer rocking her during the months she spent there in 1993.

The prosecution did point out that Tracy rode the school bus. However, this point could have been made more strongly by asking why, if Tracy was in such constant pain, her parents were forcing her to take bumpy rides on a school bus every day.

Surgery: Bane or Benefit

In both trials the defence argued that surgeries, instead of being efficacious for Tracy, made her life worse. Brayford had Laura Latimer recount Tracy's entire life, telling how each surgery made her deteriorate. Her tale held no ray of hope for her daughter. In the 1997 trial Brayford dwelt on the villainous rods inserted into Tracy's back, obviously trying to have the jury members imagine a hideous tug-of-war in Tracy's body between her twisted back and the steel rods. By having Dr. Kemp physically contort himself in a grotesque caricature of Tracy, the defence also created a vivid picture of a body too deviant from the norm to be worth salvaging. A picture, or in this case a demonstration, is worth a thousand words.

This exercise was senseless unless its underlying assumption was that medical intervention for disabled people like Tracy is unlike the same intervention for able-bodied people, that in disabled people it prolongs suffering while in able-bodied people it prolongs life. After all, the demonstration was part of the attempt to prove the necessity of this murder. However, prosecutor Neufeld, for whatever reason, didn't press for an explanation of this performance or how it was supposed to illustrate necessity.

If the reasoning implied by the defence's case were widely adopted in our society, children like Tracy would be denied all medical help. Yet the very foundation of our medical system is to help those with health problems regardless of the origin of those problems. If doctors begin to deny help to those whose lives are deemed less worthy, all citizens are at risk of some day being in Tracy Latimer's position.

Life Expectancy

The ten-year median life span cited by Dr. Dzus for children with severe cerebral palsy implied that Tracy had already lived longer than expected. However, the doctor did not say how long the ones surviving past age ten lived. Did they all die soon after that median age or did many live a long time? Were the deaths distributed from very young to middle or even old age?

The study Dr. Dzus quoted was done at the Mayo Clinic in Rochester, Minnesota but no one asked whether its findings were influenced by the United States health care system. Are Canadian parents more likely to turn to feeding tubes because of universal access to the medical system? How do Canadian study results differ from those south of the border where people may have difficulty getting health insurance for such procedures?

Dr. Kemp, the Latimers' family physician and a Crown witness, said with good care people like Tracy can live to middle age, although the

Globe and Mail quoted him saying outside the courtroom that Tracy could have died any time. Of course, so could he.

A longitudinal study of over 3,000 people with cerebral palsy reported to the British Columbia Health Surveillance Registry between 1952 and 1989 found that 87 percent of children with cerebral palsy were surviving at least to the age of thirty.[10] Almost two-thirds of children with the most severe forms of the condition and with epilepsy and the greatest mental disabilities had survived to that age. At the time these results were published the subjects had not been tracked past the age of thirty.

Because the study is ongoing no one knows how long its subjects will live. The study does mention gastrostomy feeding as one possible explanation for the lengthening life expectancy of children with cerebral palsy born in the 1980s and later, like Tracy. The results were published two years before the 1997 trial and should have been presented by the Crown. Dr. Dzus' testimony was repeated from the 1994 trial, a year before the BC study was published.

If life expectancy figures were to become justification for withdrawing medical services from, or even ending the lives of, those who survive longer than average, as the defence's case implied, then men older than seventy-five and women older than eighty-one could no longer expect help from their physicians.

Instead of Tracy's tenacious survival being respected and celebrated, it was used to justify her murder.

Tracy's Weight Loss

Much was made of Tracy's weight loss in court and in the media. Yet Laura Latimer herself said in the first trial that she and Irene Froess from the developmental centre had both disputed Tracy's last weight of forty-four and a half pounds, the most she had ever weighed. If this figure was incorrect, then all the statements made by both Brayford and Latimer himself that Tracy lost one-sixth of her body weight during that summer are also wrong.

In the second trial the evidence of Tracy's weight contradicted that of the first trial. Now her top weight was said to be forty-five pounds, taken before Tracy left for the group home in June, not after she got home in October. Tracy had probably lost weight at the group home as she had at home on other occasions but the actual loss cannot be determined accurately. In any case, a large weight loss would have benefited the defence by making her presumed suffering look worse than it was or by discounting the group home as a viable alternative for Tracy. No statistics were given in court comparing Tracy's alleged weight loss with other children like her in strange environments. Dr. Snyder did say that such children respond best when they are consistently fed the same way by the same person. If an unfamiliar environment, strange care-giving techniques or homesickness contributed to the weight loss, the situation might have been reversible. In time Tracy might have adapted to the feeding style at the group home and regained the lost weight as she had at home. Her weight loss did not necessarily discredit the group home. Both Dr. Dzus and Dr. Snyder said she probably would have eventually required a feeding tube in any case.

Regardless of the cause or her actual weight, there is no doubt that Tracy was severely underweight for a girl who was almost adult height. She weighed only about forty pounds or eighteen kilograms. The Latimers had been approached several years before Tracy's death about using a feeding tube but had rejected it.

If an able-bodied child were forced by its parents to go without food, children's services would intervene. Children from poverty-stricken areas of the world have shown that malnutrition has serious, long-term effects on physical and mental development. Yet neither prosecutor asked what effect malnutrition has on a growing body and mind or to what extent Tracy's pain, deformities and lack of alertness could be attributed to starvation.

A Humane Death?

The belief that Tracy's death was painless and humane was also based largely on flawed assumptions. Latimer said if Tracy had cried out while she was being gassed he would have taken her out of the truck, assuming that a child as weak as she would have been able to cry out in those circumstances.

In that same confession and throughout both trials there was no mention of Tracy experiencing pain during the transfer from her wheelchair to the truck nor from the passenger seat to the driver's seat. Yet Latimer also said she had pain every time she was moved. Did she not cry out as he put her in the truck or propped her up? If she did, he didn't listen so why should anyone believe his claim that he planned to take her out of the truck if she cried?

When Brayford questioned Kenneth Jones, the journeyman plumber and commercial gas fitter with SaskPower who examined the Latimer furnace and water heater, the questions tried to show how painless and humane a death this was. Under defence questioning, witnesses, such as Murray Malcolm, a toxicologist from the Regina forensic laboratory, said that carbon monoxide usually kills without victims' awareness of the danger.

Early symptoms of carbon monoxide poisoning such as headache and nausea occur only when the poisoning is slow. Malcolm concluded that Tracy died too quickly to experience any pain. No mention was made of the effects of other pollutants in exhaust fumes. Carbon monoxide may be odourless but exhaust fumes are not. They contain many other pollutants. No witnesses were ever called by the Crown in either trial to testify that Canadian animal shelters and veterinarians do not even use exhaust fumes for euthanizing animals. In my telephone conversation with him, Dr. Allan Preston, chair of the Manitoba Veterinary Medical Association's humane practices committee, said, although using exhaust from a vehicle is not illegal for killing animals, if he heard of someone doing this, he might bring charges under cruelty-to-animals legislation.

Dr. Preston told me of a study showing that animals euthanized with exhaust fumes stumble around before they die while those killed using canisters of pure compressed carbon monoxide "just lay down and go to sleep."

But the juries didn't hear such evidence and we have only the word of the person who did the killing that Tracy died painlessly. That same person had decided long before the murder that he would be willing to watch her slowly and painfully die of starvation rather than let her live with a feeding tube. Tracy's mother had agreed.

Not that painlessness should make murder acceptable. However, by ignoring the pain caused by exhaust fumes, many members of the justice system seemed willing to overlook the obvious just because they assumed any kind of death was preferable to Tracy's life.

Language

The language used by the defence to describe Tracy showed that her worth as a human being was being assessed using values that tapped into and, it would appear, harnessed bias against disabled people. These values were based on misrepresentation and exaggeration: her periodic pain became "excruciating pain;" her inability to do things for herself, everything from feeding to incontinence, was described in detail and used as evidence of suffering, terminal illness and the necessity of killing her. Not only were the positive effects of her back surgery downplayed but her last year of life was presented as "torment" living with "the horrible twisting and wrenching of her body."

The defence's description of her never-to-be surgery was grotesquely dehumanizing: "in effect sawing off the leg but cosmetically leaving it dangling there." It sounded as though her leg would not have been a part of her body, as though she had been a collection of defective body parts and the surgery would have rendered her life even less valuable than before.

In the second trial Brayford's words were even more demeaning than in the first. This time the limp leg sounded even more detached from her body. To "dangling" he added "flailing around there" and "flopping there," words which in this context sound mockingly depersonalizing.

Latimer, on the other hand, was "overwhelmingly compelled to do what he did." The motive for killing Tracy was called "normal human instinct" and "the only reasonable course." Brayford argued that lenience for his client did not mean open season on disabled people. Yet, if "normal human instincts" dictate that such a killing is "the only reasonable course," a logical conclusion would be that it is also normal to kill other disabled children who are experiencing pain. In neither trial did the prosecution call the defence to account for this terminology.

Weaknesses in Defence Unchallenged

Using the self-contradictory premise that "Bob and Laura Latimer made every single decision that was ever made by Tracy," Brayford suggested to the jury in the first trial that Robert Latimer's decision to commit murder was what his daughter wanted, that she had committed suicide by proxy: "But if in fact you were to find that this was in the best interests, that this is the decision that Tracy wanted made, that they (the Latimers) were in fact the brains that made every decision in Tracy's life, that Bob was entitled to make that decision for her and that that is the decision she wanted made I would suggest that would be another avenue." Brayford's argument was that this killing was legal because it was suicide, not assisted suicide, and suicide is not illegal.

Such a suggestion is absurd and dangerous. It assumes that, if a person is incapable of either making or communicating a decision, then the care-giver has the right to assume that the person was wishing for death and to act on that assumption. It assumes that people unable to communicate their wishes—that is, severely disabled people—want to die. Brayford's suggestion advocates bypassing the law on assisted suicide by cloaking murder of the most vulnerable as suicide.

Another weakness in the defence was the attempt to turn the premeditation into evidence of compassion.

Often a defence of mercy killing will cite emotions such as frustration to prove the stress of caring for a child like Tracy. Because they were using the necessity defence, Latimer's lawyer could not do so here. So he tried to turn an ordinarily damning description of the murder—that it was a "very considered and thoughtful and long awaited decision"[11]—into a positive one. The very evidence that should have convicted Latimer of first-degree murder was now evidence of a "loving father that was left with only one humane option." The Crown did little to take advantage of these weaknesses in the defence.

Whose Advocate was Laura?

Despite her care-giving experience, Laura Latimer appeared to be ignorant of the difference between disability and suffering. Disabled people find this is common in care-givers. A willingness to provide care does not automatically bring understanding and empathy. In fact, the care-giver role may actually work against true empathy.

In a dependency relationship such as Laura and Tracy's the two play different roles: one gives care and often is in a position of control over the other; the other receives care and traditionally defers to the control of the care-giver. As a result many care-givers cannot imagine being on the receiving end of their assistance any more than a male obstetrician, despite years of assisting births, can imagine giving birth.

Laura Latimer's depiction of her daughter's last years of life show that either she was tragically unaware of Tracy's humanity or she was willing to save her husband any way she could, even if it meant dehumanizing Tracy. She obediently followed the instructions implicit in Brayford's question. When he asked, "what kind of things developed abnormally ... as opposed to what you would expect with a newborn," she recounted all the negative events in Tracy's life, omitting anything positive, carefully substantiating the argument of necessity.

According to Laura, Tracy had been a happy little girl in her earlier years but each surgery provided nothing more than Band-Aid treatment making her life worse. In Laura's pessimistic portrait the deleterious effects of the back surgery—Tracy's rigidity and its ineffectiveness in preventing the hip dislocation—far out-weighed the health benefits of keeping food down and freedom from respiratory ailments.

Laura effectively admitted that, to her, Tracy's life was not really a life. "Her birth was way, way sadder than her death," she said. "We lost Tracy when she was born and that's—that's when I grieved for her." She apparently didn't grieve her death: "after she died I—I don't even know if I cried."

Laura's ability to nurture Tracy's intellectual needs is doubtful. She did not acknowledge the difference between linguistic comprehension and speech, which requires physical capabilities Tracy did not have and could never develop. When asked whether she had tried to follow the suggestions in the developmental centre's assessment report to simplify her language when speaking to Tracy and to encourage her to develop signals for such concepts as "stop," Laura said she had not tried to teach Tracy to talk, that Tracy couldn't talk, but that she had talked to Tracy a lot.

However, one journal entry showed that Tracy on her own had developed signals for "stop feeding me." When she was full she would screw up her face or pretend she was asleep.

It could also be argued that Laura's attitude toward Tracy's illness was as dangerous and confused as her husband's, to the point where she played a direct role in Tracy's murder. The defence used a very narrow interpretation of Laura's role to its advantage in the second trial, when Mark Brayford declared her assessment of Tracy's condition paramount because no one can know the needs of a child like the child's mother. Establishing her as the last word on Tracy's needs allowed him to use her wish for "a Kevorkian" as evidence of necessity.

A key part of the defence strategy was to set up Laura as Tracy's voice in court. Not surprisingly, Laura was defending her husband, not her dead daughter. Without the testimony of other disabled people, Tracy's voice could not really be heard. Even worse, Laura was in no real position to speak for Tracy. Her admission that she wished for a "Dr. Kevorkian" may have very well, considering her husband's emotional instability, triggered Robert Latimer's actions. He may have simply been carrying out her proposal. We can say at the very least that keeping Tracy alive was not Laura's primary concern. After all, she had also opposed using a feeding tube for her daughter, a procedure that would have eventually been necessary to keep her alive. Laura was not the advocate that Tracy deserved.

Latimer As Model Father

While he degraded Tracy, Brayford kept building up Latimer's fine character and his parenting and care-giving skills. When Brayford asked the surgeon, Dr. Dzus, about the quality of Tracy's care she concluded from her three or four office encounters with Laura and Tracy during the last year of Tracy's life, that Tracy "came from a very caring, loving environment." Yet, because of his phobia, Latimer himself avoided most of these appointments; he also did not visit Tracy while she was in intensive care.

Surely a definition of a caring, loving father does not include murder nor placing a victim's body where it could be discovered by a ten-year-old boy—Latimer put Tracy's body in the room she shared with her younger brother. A considerate father would also have realized how killing one of his children would traumatize the others.

Laura's portrait of Latimer portrayed him as a loving father to Tracy, rocking and bathing her. But no one specified whether these interactions included more than physical care, whether Tracy was encouraged to make choices, to grow and develop intellectually and in every other way.

When questioning Sergeant Robert Conlon, Brayford elicited references to Latimer's honesty, and to the notion that his behaviour toward the police differentiated him from run-of-the-mill criminals. However, the focus of the case was not Latimer's attitude and behaviour toward the police, nor even toward the rest of his family, but toward his disabled daughter. The Crown should have pointed that out.

Robert Who?

In the 1997 trial Latimer himself almost faded into the woodwork amidst all the hoopla over Tracy's physical and mental state. According to Pat Danforth, who was observing the trial, he fell asleep in court, and at one point the judge didn't notice his physical absence until the lawyers pointed out they couldn't proceed without him. His presence had become inconsequential. The proceedings were not about him; they were about Tracy. She was on trial, not he. This was a major part of the defence strategy.

Phobia

The psychiatrist who assessed Latimer for the second trial concluded that Latimer's phobia about medical devices and procedures was not pertinent to the murder because he was able to live normally and care for Tracy. However, the doctor did not say whether the Latimers' refusal of a feeding tube for Tracy was normal or whether it stemmed from Latimer's fear of medical devices. Nor did the prosecution really probe the issue or ask whether Latimer's fear of the up-coming surgery, and not Tracy's pain, triggered the murder, as his confession would suggest. Since most parents of disabled children do not kill their offspring it would appear that Latimer's actions were not normal.

Dr. Menzies was also not questioned about his knowledge of independent living options for severely disabled people, disability rights and misconceptions about disability or about his expertise on anxiety disorders such as phobias. He consulted Tracy's medical records but not evidence about her life outside medical treatment. His field is forensic psychiatry, and at least one expert, Dr. Vivienne Rowan with the St. Boniface Stress and Anxiety Clinic in Winnipeg, says people without specific training in phobias are not qualified to comment on them. Disabled activists would not consider him an expert on the so-called quality of life of a severely disabled person.

Sympathy or Justice?

Sympathy for Latimer came not only from the police, the media who bought Brayford's argument, and from the public which was getting the story second-hand as told by the media. Justice Wimmer showed that he too may have confused disability with pain in his instructions to the jury.

Tracy on Trial

To Wimmer, the judge in the 1994 trial, testimony about Tracy's disabilities was evidence of her "bleak existence" so he accepted the notion that disability is suffering. Tracy's last known weight, which Laura had said was probably incorrect, Wimmer stated as fact. Nevertheless he instructed the jury to abide by the law and the facts.

He rejected Brayford's suicide argument as "untenable" but he also disputed Kirkham's claim that the murder was a "calculated, cold-blooded murder motivated by self-interest." He called the murder a "compassionate act of kindness. That seems to be the more likely."

Judging by the jury's questioning of the judge's instructions, most of their deliberation time dealt with the definition of premeditation. Apparently they were looking for a loophole allowing a lighter sentence than the minimum of life with no parole for twenty-five years. After twice returning to the courtroom for further enlightenment from the judge, they decided the definition gave them that loophole and on November 16, 1994 pronounced Latimer not guilty of first-degree but guilty of second-degree murder and recommended the minimum prison sentence of life with no chance of parole for ten years.

In his only statement Latimer reiterated the lack of remorse he had already shown outside the courtroom, "I still feel I did what was right." To the jury who had just shown leniency toward him he said, "I don't think you people are being human."

The second jury was also sympathetic to Latimer. Although jurors are not allowed to reveal any of their deliberations, some of them were interviewed by the media. Their public statements clearly showed that they ignored evidence suggesting a motive other than compassion and fell for Brayford's emotional appeal. However, they couldn't ignore the facts entirely so they found him guilty of second-degree murder but recommended a much lighter sentence than the law allows. Their gasps on hearing the minimum sentence for second-degree murder suggest how much they had come to sympathize with the defendant and how much they had lost sight of the victim.

Justice Ted Noble was even more sympathetic toward Latimer than Wimmer had been. For weeks he deliberated, considering the minimum sentencing requirements. On December 1, 1997 he set aside concerns about the Charter rights of disabled people, ruling Latimer eligible for an unprecedented constitutional exemption. He gave him a two-year sentence, one year to be served in jail and the other on his own farm, declaring that this was an isolated case and not a signal that others could follow Latimer's lead.

The Saskatchewan Court of Appeal overturned Noble's ruling but Latimer has been given leave to appeal to the Supreme Court a second time on the grounds that the jury should have been told the minimum sentence for second-degree murder and should have been allowed to consider that he was acting as Tracy's proxy when he killed her. Alternatively he is saying that the minimum sentence of ten years is cruel and unusual punishment. The case will be heard by the court in late 1999 or early 2000. According to Bob Richards, CCD's Saskatchewan lawyer, six groups representing disabled people—CCD, The Saskatchewan Voice, DAWN Canada, People First, The Canadian Association for Community Living and PEP—are planning to submit an application for intervenor status with a supporting affidavit by the end of August 1999.

* * * * *

According to Laurie Beachell, coordinator for CCD, the first trial and the public response to it left the disabled community in shock. Both trials ignored the chilling premise on which the defence rested, that if the killing is intended to alleviate suffering and if the victim's suffering is sufficient, murder is not only acceptable; it is necessary.

Disabled people protested this premise, knowing that, as in Tracy's case, disability itself is often perceived by observers as suffering, even with no pain involved. For those with more severe forms of cerebral palsy that reaction is intensified by their involuntary facial contortions which, to the uninformed, might look like pain. This misperception about disability was borne out in these trials. In both, the defence's portrayal of the victim's discomfort confused pain with disability, mutilation and suffering.

Because the views and experiences of disabled people were omitted from both trials, the proceedings focussed less on the legality of the premise and more on the degree of Tracy's so-called suffering, whether it was enough to warrant killing her. In the first trial the Crown virtually ignored the defence treatment of Tracy, concentrating on getting a conviction but in the process giving free reign to the defence's sympathy appeal for Latimer which depended heavily on Tracy. In the second trial the constant-pain theory was disputed, Tracy's actual physical and mental competence was revealed more realistically and Latimer's options were again highlighted, as they had been in the first trial. However, while Crown prosecutor Neufeld's approach refuted many aspects of Brayford's reasoning, the defence focus on the victim's condition forced the Crown to also analyze her capabilities and thereby forced an implicit concession that, in the right circumstances, it might be necessary to kill a child like Tracy.

Tracy did not have an adequate voice in the trial. Providing such a voice was the role of the Crown, and the trial showed an abdication of the Crown's responsibility on this point. Yet we cannot simply blame the individual Crown attorneys, or—even though their case was not well argued—accuse them of basic incompetence. The trial took place in a social system that excludes the participation of disabled people in fundamental ways.

By not addressing the biased logic behind the defence's case, the prosecution limited the guilt for Tracy's death to one man—Robert Latimer. Had they paid attention to the reasoning that led to Latimer's treatment, they would have had to widen the range of guilt—to include nearly all of us who live within the biased system.

As a result, before the disabled community could fight this battle for the most basic of human rights, one they had already fought, they first had to recover from the shock of Tracy's posthumous treatment, sort out their own feelings and positions and then fight their way onto the battleground.

Tracy Latimer, an Epitaph

Tracy Lynn Latimer was a sunny girl who loved life and the simple pleasures it brought her. She was a very real little girl.

She was thrilled with parties and visits with friends and relatives. At the 1992 school Halloween party, two months after her back surgery, she wore a princess costume. When her younger sister Lindsay had a sleep-over at the Latimer house Tracy became too excited to sleep. Six months before Tracy was killed, her mother wrote in the communications book on April 3, 1993, "Tracy was the worst girl at the sleep-over, up at ten to seven, laughing and vocalizing. She was really good the rest of the day. Lindsay read to her."

On about April 11, 1993, Easter Sunday, Laura wrote, "Brian and Lindsay got up at 5:30 a.m. to hunt for eggs. We spent most of Easter day at Tracy's cousin Lynn's place.... There were lots of cousins and kids, and grandma and grandpa were there. Tracy spent a happy day, she ate a nice supper, and really enjoyed the des[s]erts."[12]

Tracy liked watching hockey on TV. When she and the other children at the developmental centre played clapping games she would try to keep them going after they stopped. On October 4, the day after she got home from a three-month stay in a North Battleford group home—during which time there were no entries in the book—and just three weeks before her death, her mother wrote: "The green badges on Tracy's tray are what she won at bowling, she did the best in her class."

She took the school bus daily with the other children to Wilkie sixteen kilometres away. On May 23, 1993 the Latimers went on a supper picnic at Finlayson Island with friends and took Tracy along. Laura wrote to the school, "Wannell's picked us up in their motor home. Tracy went in her wheelchair, and we used tie downs to strap her in.

She seemed tickled with the outing, ate a very good supper, especially enjoyed lemon pie for des[s]ert. She slept on the bed in the motor home on the way back, had milk and pudding at bedtime."

Apparently she was not sleepless from pain after the back surgery. Contrary to her mother's testimony at the trials she could sleep even in a strange bed in a moving vehicle that would have rocked or jostled her. Nor was she uninterested in food.

A May 1993 assessment said she "enjoys cause/effect toys, she has a pull switch and manipulates a switchboard to activate toys." She liked the sounds of the bells and toys attached to her wheelchair. Laura's May 5, 1993 entry in the communications book said, "She loved the bells. I gave Brian heck, because I thought he was hitting his glass with a pen. We laughed when I realized it was Tracy and her bells."

As a witness Laura tried to downplay her daughter's ability to choose but Tracy had definite preferences. When Lindsay would put an array of nail polish bottles in front of her she invariably chose red.

The soft touch of a kitten's fur prompted her to try picking it up. The May report's clinical shorthand quoted Laura as saying, "She will try to pat, pick up the cat" and "Tracy smiles when she sees the cat." Like other children, she liked the warmth of a hug and being rocked. The dancing flames of a bonfire mesmerized her.

And there was a streak of mischief behind those eyes. Whenever her left hand was within range of a bespectacled person like her father, the doctor or people at the developmental centre, she would pull the glasses off, throw them on the floor and teasingly turn back for a reaction.

It was true that Tracy had cerebral palsy, that she had experienced pain and would have encountered more but it was not true that it was constant or excruciating as Laura's testimony said. Like other children disabled at birth, Tracy knew no other life. This was the life she had been given and she enjoyed it, valued it and fought to keep it, just as most able-bodied people value their lives.

The communications book entries written by Laura and read for the Crown during the second trial showed Tracy relished these simple pleasures at least until Tuesday, October 19, the date of the last entry, five days before her life was taken from her. Laura's entry that day read, "Tracy was good, ate and drank fine Tracy was good, ate really well, had a bath, Bob bathed her." It was the day Robert Latimer decided on using exhaust fumes to kill her.

In able-bodied people pain is a symptom, but in Tracy it was a death sentence carried out by her father and condoned by her mother, the defence attorney, the judges and juries and most media and their audiences. It was not her intermittent pain that was the predominant issue in either trial. It was her disability. Because she couldn't speak, the assumption was that she couldn't comprehend and, if she couldn't comprehend, her death really wasn't as monstrous as the killing of someone who could.

Tracy could understand much more than she was given credit for and she clearly had a voice. Even without speech she communicated more than pain. Her smiles said she was happy most of the time. The May 1993 report said she "smiles broadly in response to game," that her eyes got big when the staff at the centre put cream on her hands. It also said, "Mrs. Latimer indicated that Tracy does vocalize at home, mostly pleasure… she is very sociable…. She liked her family, she likes people…. When she is full she'll screw up her face or pretend she's asleep."

The police, the court and the media refused to hear that voice. Her mother heard it but then denied it. Her father took her voice away.

Tracy Lynn Latimer
born Sunday, November 23, 1980
died Sunday, October 24, 1993
age 12 years, 11 months

Notes

1. Details about the murder and trial were taken from the transcripts of Robert Latimer's two trials: *R. v. Robert W. Latimer* (1994) and (1997).
2. See Chapter Four.
3. Parentheses are the author's.
4. Details about the murder and the events of the following days came from Latimer's confession and the testimonies of Constable Nick Hartle, Sergeant Robert Conlon and Corporal Kenneth Lyons. Robert Latimer, the accused, did not testify in either trial, as is the case in almost all murder trials.
5. Georgina Heselton. June 20, 1998. Telephone interview.
6. Council of Canadians With Disabilities. CCD Policy Resolutions.
7. In May 1993, when the Rodriguez case reached the Supreme Court, CCD was known as the Council of Provincial Organizations of the Handicapped or COPOH. See Chapter Three for the reasons behind the name change.
8. Dick Sobsey, "The Media and Robert Latimer," p. 28.
9. Alanna Mitchell (October 26, 1995). "Latimer entitled to new trial." The *Globe and Mail*, A2.
10. See Appendix A.
11. J.U. Crichton et. al "The Life-Expectancy of Persons with Cerebral Palsy."
12. For Laura's entries in the communications book as transcribed into the records of Robert Latimer's second trial, see Appendix A. The report referred to in the epitaph was also in the court transcripts as were any other details not included in Laura's written account.

Chapter Two

The Media Trial

A major obstacle impeding the disabled community's access to the battleground over the Latimer case was media coverage. Not only were disabled spokespeople excluded from the courtroom, they were also largely excluded from the public debate on assisted suicide and euthanasia raging in newspapers, on television and on radio. By the time many had recovered from their shock enough to organize a forceful protest the story had already been framed in a way that connected Latimer with euthanasia, and euthanasia with disability. As we will see, these assumptions—which are based on a serious misunderstanding of disability—were established early on and changed little throughout the trial.

The disabled community pointed out these links, but in the media both euthanasia and disability had other connotations. To disabled advocates euthanasia was the negative factor while in the media it was treated as a rational, humane option to life with disability. To disabled advocates disability is a fact of life that sometimes brings pain but is certainly not synonymous with it while in the media disability was treated as an acceptable excuse for homicide. Yet, as shown by the quotes they used and by the sources to which they turned, the media denied or ignored the disability element in the case. From the beginning the shape the story took in the media was based on several significant assumptions: that Tracy's disabilities meant she was in constant pain; that her murder was an example of mercy killing or euthanasia; and that the victim in the case was Robert Latimer, not his daughter.

The Starting Point

The way a news story will be framed is determined very early on. As veteran reporters know, once a story line has taken hold it is very difficult to get it recast, and this is as true on the streets as it is in newsrooms. People usually prefer to make new information fit the original story line rather than question the initial assumptions, losing what George Orwell called the struggle to see what is in front of one's nose. The story line in the Latimer case was established even before Robert Latimer's first trial. Before anything had been proven in court and when Latimer's compassionate motives were nothing more than the defence's

48

claims, the media linked the story with mercy killing and euthanasia. The second paragraph of a Canadian Press story printed in the *Chronicle Herald* on November 7, 1994, the first day of the first trial, said, "The case ... comes amid a national debate on the issues of euthanasia and mercy killing."[1] Later the article also said, "Topics such as euthanasia and mercy killing are being debated by Canadians through forums such as a Commons committee established earlier this year."

This piece also paraphrased a spokesperson for the Ontario Federation for Cerebral Palsy, who said, "the case is an important part of a broader discussion on the ethics and morality of caring for the disabled." Already, the case was being thought of less as a murder trial than as a forum for considering ideas such as Latimer's claim that killing Tracy was a reasonable alternative to surgery.

The starting point in the Latimer coverage also emphasized disability. This early CP article, typical of what followed even after the trial ended, elided Tracy's pain in favour of her disability. Its headline read, "Farmer on trial in disabled daughter's killing." The article itself quoted Mark Brayford describing Tracy's disabilities: "This child could not roll over on its own. This child would be in diapers." No source was asked to comment on the dehumanizing implications of the pronoun, "its." The headline and this quote, left without any opposing view, supported the impression that Tracy's disabilities rendered her subhuman and warranted her murder.

The story didn't mention Tracy's dislocated hip or any pain. It did say three times that Tracy "suffered from cerebral palsy." However, as was discussed in the previous chapter, suffering has become an almost meaningless word referring to a very wide range of negative experiences. Because the lives of people with cerebral palsy are filled with many positive experiences, not just pain, "suffering" was misleading.

The article described cerebral palsy, not in terms of pain, but only by the disabilities it causes: a person with cerebral palsy "moves in a jerky or spastic manner"; "has trouble speaking"; "lack(s) muscle coordination"; is "someone in a wheelchair who must be spoon-fed." Therefore, the phrase "suffered from cerebral palsy" referred to disability, not pain. Because the article focussed on disability when it described cerebral palsy but failed to say that people with that condition can still lead fulfilled lives, it also implied that disability makes life totally negative and therefore synonymous with suffering, whether there is physical pain or not. Pain was absent from the article, which did not question whether, if the victim had not been disabled, pain would have justified killing her. Because the Canadian Press news service, where this story originated, is used extensively by media outlets across the country, this one story had a much wider audience than just the *Chronicle Herald* readership.

A Voice Unheard

Disabled advocates objected to the coverage but received a defensive response. On November 19, 1994 just after the first trial, a brief story appeared in the Saskatoon *Star Phoenix* about disabled advocates criticizing media descriptions of Tracy Latimer.[2] Mel Graham of the Council of Canadians with Disabilities was quoted saying, "'I would have liked a paragraph or two ... outlining what other families have done with children who are severely physically and intellectually disabled.'" He also said such stories should have been run before public opinion crystallized.

It was a reasonable request for balance but the article countered with lawyer Anne Wallace saying the media should exercise caution in selecting stories to run while a case is before the courts. "'If you start doing this sort of thing it may be construed as an attempt to influence the outcome (of the trial),' said Wallace."

In other cases involving vulnerable people, the media have gone out of their way to balance or even correct public misperceptions about that group or individual and they have criticized judge's statements, even if they waited until well after a trial to do it. When David Milgaard and his mother, Joyce, finally managed to convince a few journalists that his conviction and imprisonment had been a horrible mistake, those journalists went to bat for him, writing stories showing another interpretation of the Gail Miller murder than the one the courts had accepted. Joyce Milgaard has said publicly that she couldn't have won the battle without this support.

The media do not have to blindly, blandly report only the court proceedings. They can and often do provide background material to give their stories context and enhance their audiences' understanding. So they did not have to report only what they were hearing about Tracy from Latimer's team. Yet even before the case went to court, the media had basically accepted the line of reasoning that the defence would use. Even if journalists had to restrict themselves to court proceedings during the trial, they could have provided better balance and a more representative portrayal of people with cerebral palsy, both before and after the trial.

In order to do that they would have had to consult those with first-hand understanding of disability issues. Already at the pre-trial stage it was evident that, despite the media's own constant references to disability, they had little intention of turning to those who could testify to a life with a disability like Tracy's. Instead they turned to those who could testify to Robert and Laura Latimer's perspective. Several times the November 7 Canadian Press story referred to "advocates for the disabled" and quoted a spokesperson for the Ontario Federation for Cerebral Palsy but made no mention of advocates who were themselves disabled—a telling distinction. It was a distinction that kept disabled advocates on the sidelines, as voiceless as Tracy had been.

From Assisted Suicide to Mercy Killing

While the CP article of November 7 referred to the heated debate about euthanasia and mercy killing, it did not say that, until the Latimer case, the debate had been most heated during Sue Rodriguez' struggle for an individual exemption from the law against assisted suicide. She wanted the aid of a physician in ending her life when and how she chose and her major concern was autonomy. Rodriguez lost her Supreme Court appeal just days before Robert Latimer decided to kill Tracy; he carried out his plan less than a month after that narrow defeat. Latimer himself made the link between himself, Rodriguez and mercy killing by arguing that his status as Tracy's care-giver and his compassionate motives made Tracy's murder another assisted suicide.

At the time of his arrest few if any media outside the province paid much attention to this little story from backwoods Saskatchewan. The available 1993 print coverage from Saskatoon was neutral compared with what followed a year later. However, the first indications of a shift away from balanced coverage and toward Latimer's version of events occurred soon after the arrest.

Originally the *Star Phoenix* followed standard journalistic style guidelines by not including features separating members of a minority group from the mainstream population unless relevant to the story. Its coverage of Latimer's arrest did not mention Tracy's disabilities. The headline on November 5, 1993 simply said, "Man accused of murdering daughter to appear in court."[3] The copy described her as Latimer's twelve-year-old daughter, "severely affected by cerebral palsy" and didn't mention her pain, although in a following story the same paper said she had twenty-four-hour pain, which was later proven to be untrue.

Five days after the first story in the *Star Phoenix,* the Regina *Leader Post* picked it up, condensing it to a brief filler. Here she was Latimer's "12-year-old disabled daughter" and she no longer was "severely affected by" but "suffered from" cerebral palsy.[4] In the first phrase cerebral palsy was simply an effect on Tracy; in the second the presumed effect was labeled suffering. That so-called suffering was to become a major theme inside and outside the courtroom.

During this phase Latimer's lawyer, Richard Gibbons, from North Battleford, defended his client by stressing the burden of caring for Tracy. On November 12, 1993 he told The *Star Phoenix*: "Yet to say Latimer … believes compassion is a defence for first-degree murder is oversimplifying the case."[5] The article said Gibbons didn't use the term "mercy killing" but did emphasize the "strains, stresses and tremendous pressure experienced by a family caring for a person with multiple handicaps." Gibbons, apparently recognizing the importance of framing the case in the media, went on the offensive.

The *Star Phoenix* said, "Robert Latimer isn't some sort of monster.... But Gibbons believes that's what some people may conclude after the media coverage since his client was arrested."

After Latimer had changed lawyers, the defence changed. Mark Brayford suggested a jury could disregard evidence pointing to first-degree murder. The *Star Phoenix* duly reported this: "What superficially might appear to be a crime may not be once 12 jurors sit down and apply their common sense to it. Jurors don't have to give reasons and they take a look at the big picture."[6] Instead of arguing stress and burden he planned to ask the jury to ignore the law. Yet the *Star Phoenix* journalist did not challenge Brayford on this point. Neither did most others.

Brayford's tactics seemed to bring more positive results for his client in the media than Gibbon's. Three weeks after Brayford took over, less than two months after the murder, Saskatoon CBC TV featured a one-hour interview with the Latimers which became evidence in both trials. Several newspapers reported from their viewing of the video in court that in it Latimer was already talking about the growing public support for his cause.

The place this murder occupied in the euthanasia debate was fixed long before the first trial began.

This conceptual shift from assisted suicide as the autonomous actions of competent, verbal adults to the murder of a non-verbal child was exactly what The Council of Canadians with Disabilities and People in Equal Participation had feared when they made their presentations on assisted suicide to the Supreme Court. Rodriguez' autonomy was at the heart of her struggle. Tracy's autonomy was completely disregarded. The media failed to call attention to this fundamental difference.

A Negative Bias

The coverage of the Latimer case showed the same prevailing bias about disability so evident in court. Beatrice A. Wright, psychologist and author, has identified three factors in establishing such a negative bias: "if ... something is perceived as negative ... and stands out ... in a sparse context (internal or external), then the psychological events that follow will assume a negative course."[7]

In the typical approach to the story, disability stood out as Tracy's only salient feature. The first impression readers got of her was her disability. References to her cerebral palsy were also about disability:

the symptoms of the condition included only disabilities. There was rarely any discussion of whether Tracy was indeed in pain, or the positive, enjoyable parts of her life.

The descriptions of Tracy's disability generally listed all the things people like her cannot do. She was described, not as simply having cerebral palsy, but "suffering" from it. Since only 10 percent of people with this condition are as severely affected as Tracy, and the condition does not automatically bring a life of suffering even for those who are severely affected, saying that Tracy "suffered from cerebral palsy" shows the negative perception of cerebral palsy. There was rarely any mention of the many accomplishments of people like Tracy.

The third aspect of the negative bias was also widely present . Omitting Tracy's abilities and pleasures and showing her disabilities as her only noteworthy feature placed her in a sparse context, preventing readers from seeing anything else about her, from seeing her as a human being. And in this process, as Brayford's language revealed, she became an "it," less human than other murder victims.

The presence of these three components at an early stage in the coverage showed a negative bias against the victim of this murder, even before the court had made any decision about Latimer's claim of compassion and the necessity of the murder.

Dispensing News

The sharing of news across the country was a factor in the Latimer coverage. Most daily newspapers rely heavily on the Canadian Press or other news services to cover stories they can't or choose not to cover themselves. During the first Latimer trial the service of choice was the CP.

The Canadian Press is a national news co-operative of daily newspapers incorporated in 1910 and headquartered in Toronto while its French-language operations, La Presse Canadienne (PC) and Nouvelles Télé-Radio (NTR) are directed from Montréal. CP news, available by subscription to corporations, individuals, government offices, broadcasters and newspapers, supplies large newspapers with about 300 columns of news and 150 photos a day while smaller newspapers receive a service tailored to regional readership.

For the following analysis five daily newspapers from across Canada were chosen on the basis of their ongoing inclusion in the *Canadian Index*. A sixth, the Saskatoon *Star Phoenix*, was absent from the index but was searched manually to provide a local picture. A few 1993 Regina *Leader Post* articles showed when the story was picked up in other parts of that province.

Radio samples were mostly unavailable but a few television interviews were included. Two were of CBC's *The Magazine* from 1997—an interview of the Latimers by Hana Gartner and a follow-up show including numerous guests speaking on a variety of topics related to the unusual constitutional exemption. *Maclean's* also ran a number of articles. A few Winnipeg television news broadcasts from Latimer's 1998 appeal provided a more recent picture of the coverage.

A computer search of the first trial coverage in the five newspapers combined with a manual search of the *Star Phoenix* revealed eighty articles and commentaries between Monday, November 7 to Christmas Eve 1994. Of these articles thirty-five, or 44 percent, were supplied by CP of which only one was augmented by the paper's—the *Globe and Mail's*—own writer.

Newspapers outside Saskatchewan were understandably the most dependent on CP. The Halifax *Chronicle Herald* turned to the wires for eleven of twelve stories, the Calgary *Herald* for nine of thirteen articles and the Montreal *Gazette* for seven of nine stories. The Vancouver *Sun* had a total of only four, two from CP. In these four publications an average of 71 percent—twenty-seven of thirty-eight articles—originated with this news co-operative.

The *Globe and Mail* clearly sent its own staff to cover the event. Only five of its twenty stories were entirely or partly done by CP. The *Star Phoenix* from Saskatoon, the nearest city to North Battleford and Wilkie, also covered the trial itself. It was the most prolific with thirty-two stories of which only four came from CP and one from the Regina *Leader Post*.

Because so many daily newspapers and broadcasters subscribe to and use CP services extensively, this one source carries a huge responsibility for informing Canadians, a responsibility which carries considerable clout and risk. Although all of the newspapers in the eighty-article sample wrote very similar pieces even when they were writing their own material, phrases and descriptions apparently originating with CP filtered into stories not from CP. A notably persistent example, that Tracy Latimer "couldn't walk, talk or feed herself" appeared in Brent Jang's CP article in the Calgary *Herald* on Wednesday, November 9, 1994, just two days after the trial began. The phrase surfaced in newspaper after newspaper, broadcast after broadcast, year after year. It was still going strong in 1998.

On November 25, 1997, three years after it was first used, CBC TV's Hana Gartner resurrected this tired refrain to describe Tracy in the introduction to her interview with the Latimers. And in the October 1998 coverage of Latimer's second appeal in Saskatchewan, it appeared yet again. Significantly, it has nothing to do with the pain supposedly pivotal to Latimer's necessity defence but everything to do with disability. Yet it became one of the stock descriptions of Tracy.

Headlines and Content

Newspaper reporters generally do not write their own headlines, and the headline is one of the few parts of a CP story that subscribing papers change. As such, headlines alone do not necessarily reflect the real nature of a news article—they are designed to be provocative, and to grab the attention of readers. Yet one of the ways they do this is by relying on the way a story has come to be framed. As a news story develops, a certain vocabulary of words and phrases becomes associated with it. In Tracy's case, an example is the phrase "couldn't walk, talk, or feed herself." Headline writers draw on this pool of phrases, triggering the reader's familiarity with the story. This process supports the story line as it has come to be written.

The eighty headline samples for the 1994 trial and post-trial period suggest the extent to which the media's account of events was inaccurate, driven more by the internal logic of the story line that had developed than by reality.

Although in court the dissection of Tracy's body into its imperfect parts occupied a significant portion of the trial, in the media coverage she was less significant than the person who had killed her. Of the eighty headlines only twenty-five mentioned or alluded to Tracy. Of those, only seven identified her simply by name or as a daughter, girl or child: for example, "Dad found guilty of killing daughter."[8] Only three of eighty headlines referred to Tracy without some negative qualifier, as in the CP article in the Montreal *Gazette,* "Father had no choice but to kill girl: lawyer," (November 16, 1994.)[9]

Many headlines described Tracy as disabled. A CP story in the *Globe and Mail* was headed, "Farmer accused of killing his disabled daughter"[10] and another CP story in the same newspaper was titled, "Mother describes disabled girl's life."[11] In total 90 percent of these headlines linked Tracy with her disabilities or the less-than-enviable aspects of her life.

The headlines were generally consistent with the way the defence collapsed Tracy's disability into pain. Only three headlines referred to her pain, supposedly the basis of Latimer's necessity defence, and all three were quotes from either Robert or Laura Latimer, such as the CP story headed, "'My priority was to put her out of pain,' sobbing father said"[12] or "Death ended pain, mom says."[13]

One headline from the *Globe and Mail* said, "Palsy victims can live into 30s, doctor testifies," but a sub-head dashed that solitary beacon of hope: "Latimer girl was in danger of dying at any time, he says outside court."[14] This was a speculative and highly debatable opinion that should have been balanced in the story by someone with equal qualifications giving an opposing view. There was none.

A Voice Unheard

No headlines included anything about Tracy other than her disabilities. Her likes and dislikes, her interactions with her siblings and other people, her playfulness and smiles—such descriptions directly refuted the necessity argument and therefore were central to the case. Yet all were omitted.

Robert Latimer fared much better in the headlines than did Tracy. In court his role was understated. He did not testify and his lawyer produced no witnesses. Doctors' and Laura Latimer's testimonies, which provided the preponderance of defence evidence, centred around Tracy's body, not around the defendant even though he was technically the one on trial. In the media, however, Latimer got 60 percent more headlines than Tracy and while descriptions of her were consistently negative, the descriptions of her killer were positive or neutral. The same process that can produce a negative bias can also produce a positive one if the outstanding feature is valued.

Latimer was usually identified simply by his last name but the next favourite descriptors emphasized his place in the community and in his family: "Father had no choice but to kill girl: lawyer,"[15] for example. Of the forty headlines mentioning him specifically, half connected him to his home life; thirteen referred to him as a father or dad; an additional three were about the Latimer family; another four called him a farmer.

Seven pointed out his kindness or his humane treatment of Tracy while he was killing her, for example that he was poised to take her out of the truck if she cried out: "Latimer confessed, say police" with the sub-head, "'If she had started to cry, I would have taken her out of there'."[16] Two said he was honest or even too honest: "Murder sentence stirs angry waves across the nation" with the sub-head, "Farmer may have been penalized for being too honest, professor says."[17] His previous encounters with the law rated only a paragraph or two in a *Globe and Mail* article and in the Calgary *Herald* but this side of him did not appear in the headlines. Only one called him a killer and that was inside a quote from the Civil Liberties Association demanding his release: "'Revoke killer's sentence' Civil Liberties Association wants Latimer released."[18] While it was not a professional error in judgement to humanize the defendant, such treatment should have been balanced by equally humanizing treatment of the victim. That it was not showed that the media had adopted a line on the story, and were sticking with it, biased or not.

While news headlines should not influence a case in court, they undoubtedly affect public opinion. Headlines fanned the flames of public support for Latimer. Almost one-third trumpeted public support for Latimer in the form of petitions to free him, to diminish his sentence or to demand a change in the minimum sentencing laws. One even said strangers were phoning the Latimers asking for advice.[19]

The Media Trial

After the trial the headlines were more concerned about the perceived hardships of the convicted murderer than about justice for his victim, as in "Justice system lacks compassion for Latimer."[20] Another CP article in the *Chronicle Herald*, "Latimer copes with publicity,"[21] turned the favourable publicity into a burden for Latimer. In the Vancouver *Sun's* "Father's 'tragic conundrum'"[22] the tragedy was from Latimer's perspective, not Tracy's.

Despite the fact that mercy killing as such was not the topic in court, it got high ratings in the headlines: nearly half mentioned euthanasia or assisted suicide. None talked about the necessity defence or how it differs from euthanasia.

Debating mercy killing was not the purpose of the trial. It was supposed to determine Robert Latimer's guilt or innocence in this crime of pre-meditated murder. Few of the headlines posed the question of murder versus mercy killing and the stories did not probe whether this case really qualified as mercy killing.

By comparison, the opposition to lenience for Latimer got only ten of the eighty headlines. Two of these were editorials saying mercy killing is murder but not questioning whether this was a mercy killing: "Mercy killing is murder; Law should not change because of exceptional case."[23]

Despite their emphasis on disability, a mere four of the eighty headlines featured responses from a disability perspective. One lonely headline in the Montreal *Gazette* asked readers to gauge Tracy on the same basis as an able-bodied child: "A simple test: What if Tracy Latimer had been a healthy girl?"[24]

The end of the trial brought a torrent of media coverage peaking with eighteen articles on November 18, 1994, eleven of them in the *Star Phoenix*. Much of it connected this case with the issues of assisted suicide and mercy killing; none asked whether justice had been done for Tracy.

The CP story comparing Tracy and Sue Rodriguez was picked up by the *Star Phoenix* and the Calgary *Herald*. Both included the child and the adult in the same headline. Although the articles quoted a Member of Parliament saying the two cases were not alike, the simple fact that they appeared in the same headlines suggests a link. Otherwise why mention it? That MP's statement might have been valid as a tiny aside in the story but not in the headlines.

The bias shown in the news headlines no doubt contributed to the way the story grabbed the attention of Canadians and many supported the convicted killer with money and letters. This support received a good deal of coverage. "Sympathy growing for Latimer family: Cash, gifts and support letters flow into home."[25] Little money flowed the way of disability rights groups.

Language

On November 19, 1994 the *Star Phoenix* took the unusual step of defending in print its description of Tracy Latimer by claiming to be following guidelines set by style books. Although its initial descriptions of Tracy were indeed better than what followed a year later, it eventually was indistinguishable from other publications.

The latest style guides recommend identifying members of minority groups as people, not by the features differentiating them from the mainstream population. Those differences should appear only when they are relevant to the story. As such it was legitimate to mention Tracy's disability but only in the context of the alleged motive, as the cause of the supposedly unrelenting pain the defence was using to vindicate the murder.

However, descriptions of Tracy's disabilities and so-called suffering used before, during and after the first trial were no longer mere sideline adjectives helping readers understand the situation. Her deformities and disabilities dominated her portrayal in the media. Little else was said about her by the Latimers or trial witnesses and few if any journalists questioned this as they would have for negative descriptors of other minority groups.

Protests had little effect on the singularly uniform, dismissive coverage of the victim. On November 19, 1994 the *Star Phoenix* reported disabled people's disapproval of the descriptions of Tracy[26] but everywhere the disparaging chant continued—Tracy couldn't walk, talk or feed herself; she was in constant pain; she had cerebral palsy since birth; she suffered; she was severely disabled.

Television and radio coverage were no better. Hanna Gartner's interview with the Latimers on November 25, 1997 was particularly bad. Gartner focussed on Tracy's inability to "walk, talk or feed herself" without explaining the relevance of this phrase to the case.[27] In her introduction to the interview she said, "He killed his disabled daughter. Now Robert Latimer faces a life sentence." Without an explanation of the relevance of disability to the case, it sounded as though Tracy's disabilities had been Latimer's reason for killing her and as though he was being unjustly punished. Of the three people who appeared in that episode of *The Magazine*—she and the Latimers—she was the only one who used the word disabled. Yet a week later when the disability aspect of the case was pointed out to her, she quoted Justice Noble saying in his ruling that this wasn't about disability.[28]

Just as in the headlines, the articles in the print media also repeatedly portrayed Tracy as little more than disabled, severely disabled or as suffering from cerebral palsy. They concentrated on her low level of mental ability, her need for diapering and other personal care. Reporting an interview with one of the witnesses, Dr. Richard Snyder, the *Globe and Mail* reiterated Tracy's defects which had already been covered in another article on the same day: "with her degree of brain damage Tracy was always in danger of death;" she "had many seizures;" she was "mentally retarded as well as physically disabled;" she had "no control over her arms and legs and was involuntarily jerky;" "She needed to be spoon-fed and diapered and could not get to a sitting position by herself;" she "had lost a great deal of weight."[29] If it was all right to bolster her negative image with interviews outside the court, surely this article could have included testimonials to the positive parts of her life.

A CP story in the Calgary *Herald* described Tracy as "a disabled girl," who "couldn't walk, talk or feed herself," "had little or no control over her muscles," and had "suffered from cerebral palsy since birth." The language used in this story was typical of the way Tracy was described: "strapped to a wheelchair and needing to be spoon-fed;" "victim;" "needed constant care;" "had seizures;" "wearing diapers."[30]

If the pain was included, it was usually described as constant pain. Alternatively, pain seemed incidental, sometimes placed at the end of a piece like an afterthought. The Calgary *Herald* article's only reference to pain came in its last words, "the pain that Tracy endured" in a sentence describing Latimer's concern for his daughter.[31]

Latimer was treated as kindly in the stories as in the headlines. Depictions of him highlighted his positive personality traits, sometimes inferring them from minimal evidence. Judging by Latimer's appearances on television he could easily have been described as plodding and inarticulate but The *Star Phoenix* preferred to say he was "calm and controlled but a little distant."[32] Rather than emphasize the cold way he timed his daughter's death or his awareness of his criminal culpability when he destroyed evidence and made her body look like she died in her sleep, journalists said he "sobbed to police"[33] or made a "tearful confession."[34]

The Canadian Press said he was a caring, loving man so that was how he appeared in all the newspapers using those stories. He was a "loving father"[35] who "spent years spoon-feeding his ... daughter."[36] In reality Laura did most of the feeding. Rather than simply saying the police led him away they added positive descriptors: the police "led a stoic Latimer away ... not in handcuffs."[37]

The descriptions of the crime itself were another telling clue to the writers' attitudes. Journalists avoided the term "murder" to describe the act. Murder was used only for the charges against Latimer or his convictions. The journalists consistently described the actual murder as a killing, a word easily paired with "mercy" and which often was. Kill also does not carry the connotations of culpability implicit in murder although in the Gartner interview Latimer objected even to that word. He wanted people to say he had "helped" Tracy.

Instead of murder, the story employed euphemisms such as Tracy died in her sleep or even was put out of her pain, a phrase usually reserved for animals. The *Star Phoenix* announced the guilty verdict in a piece that led off, "A Battleford jury has convicted Robert Latimer, 41, of second-degree murder in the death of his 12-year-old daughter." The sentence separates "murder" from "death."[38] It could have been shortened to conform to journalistic standards of conciseness by saying instead, "has convicted Robert Latimer, 41, of the second-degree murder of his 12-year-old daughter."

While the *Chronicle Herald* headline for that same day simply said, "Dad found guilty of killing daughter," the accompanying CP article's lead paragraph said, "A father who spent years spoon-feeding his disabled daughter before venting exhaust fumes to end her life was found guilty Wednesday of second-degree murder."[39] Besides the factual error about spoon-feeding, this sentence made Latimer sound like the aggrieved, long-suffering care-giver and also separated the murder conviction from the act. As in the *Star Phoenix*, this made the actual killing sound like something other than murder.

The brutality of the murder itself was further softened by repeated reference to Latimer's claim that "he was poised to stop the engine"[40] instead of suggesting how inhumane it was for a father to time his daughter's death and calmly watch her being sent into spasms by the exhaust fumes he was force-feeding her. Journalists had only the word of the killer that he would have stopped the engine if she had cried out and they didn't investigate whether a child as weak as she would have been able to cry out in those circumstances. The fact that he didn't take her out was ignored.

Tracy's murder should have been acknowledged as such.

Structure

The structure of the articles was equally slanted. Typically, after the lead paragraph, the first quote was either Robert Latimer or someone speaking on his behalf. This occurred even after he was first convicted of second-degree murder.

Defence counsel Mark Brayford was given a prominent place and the total amount of space given pro-Latimer sources always dominated the stories. When the two lawyers gave their closing arguments after the 1994 trial, the *Star Phoenix* ran the story split between the first and second pages. Brayford was covered on the front page while Crown counsel Randy Kirkham got the last few lines on the first page where his account was described as an "attack." Most of his argument was buried on the inside page.[41]

A brief eight-paragraph CP story in the *Chronicle Herald* on November 16, 1994 gave the first five paragraphs to Brayford's closing arguments and the last two to Kirkham. A two-line paragraph between the two sources described Tracy as having had "severe cerebral palsy since birth."[42]

The Gartner interview gave no time to anyone but the Latimers and other interviews aired the day of the sentencing included only one disabled person, Catherine Frazee. The questions posed to her didn't give her an opportunity to speak on how this case affected disabled people; one question asked how long she thought Latimer's sentence should be. The guests commenting about the effects on disabled people were all able-bodied care-givers, most of them sympathetic to the views of disabled activists but nevertheless unable to speak from experience.

Again, the defence and support for Latimer were more important than anything said by opponents. Tracy, the victim, had no one to speak for her.

Sources

Invariably the sources quoted in the news stories were the same: the defendant and his supportive wife, medical professionals who had seen Tracy at the lowest points in her life and were in no position to testify to her life as a whole, and the police, at least one of whom knew "Bob" Latimer socially. An occasional neighbour was cornered for an opinion but it was painfully obvious that the neighbours did not know Tracy except as the Latimer's burdensome child. One of them concluded she must have been in a lot of pain because she was having so many surgeries.[43] An occasional piece quoted a spokesperson for some organization or other but the people who knew Tracy at the developmental centre or the group home were hardly consulted, if at all.

In spite of the constant references to disability, the comparisons to the severely disabled Sue Rodriguez and the obvious connection between disabled people and assisted suicide—only severely disabled people cannot commit suicide without help—people with those disabilities were consulted only rarely. Those living with Tracy's condition and others like it were largely ignored. The citizens most vulnerable to the effects of this campaign were shunted aside.

Those few disabled people who agreed with Latimer were sought out and given more prominent space as in the November 17, 1997 series in *Maclean's* where Latimer's disabled cousin got the first paragraphs. Those opposing him were buried deep in the stories or relegated to the end.[44] This treatment ignored the fact that, nation-wide, most organizations of disabled people opposed Latimer. The national umbrella group, the Council of Canadians with Disabilities, which represents several hundred thousand disabled members, had reversed its early reserved support for Rodriguez in light of the danger revealed by the Latimer case.

Even after the second trial the media didn't look for Canadian evidence on the life expectancy of children like Tracy or probe the validity of the single American study cited by Dr. Dzus and Dr. Snyder. They didn't question Brayford's brazen and sinister assumption that, because Tracy's parents had always made all decisions about her welfare while she was alive that the accused had been acting as her proxy when he killed her.

They didn't question the statements of expert witnesses like Tracy's doctors who would have seen her only when she was in trouble. Tracy's lack of smiles for her doctors were cited as evidence that she couldn't recognize people but perhaps her smiles for them didn't come as readily as for family, friends and the staff at the developmental centre because she did indeed recognize doctors and associated them with painful procedures.

Obviously the journalist from the Star Phoenix who first wrote about Tracy's twenty-four-hour pain didn't bother to check out the type or duration of that pain by interviewing sources other than the defence team. Surely the writer knew that using only the confessed murderer, his lawyer and their supporters would yield nothing but a rerun of Latimer's version of the story.

Instead journalists opted in favour of the defendant by choosing those sources belabouring the horror of Tracy's care requirements and her disabilities, sources who would highlight the wish of some disabled people to end their lives.

Tunnel Vision

Once the media had chosen the story line, the result was tunnel vision that blacked out other possible motives and explanations for the murder.

Hana Gartner claimed Tracy was in "constant pain," an argument the Crown had challenged with compelling evidence just days before the interview aired. And Latimer talked about cutting and mutilation more than pain. He seemed obsessed with the "cutting" part of the surgery he had "helped" Tracy avoid. When he spoke about Tracy's pain he spoke of the "torture" of the cutting and "sawing" she was to have endured. It sounded as though she was to have endured this "mutilation," as he called it, without anesthetic.

Several times he agitatedly launched into tirades about the cruelty of cutting feeding tubes into Tracy and "cutting this and cutting that." In the quarter hour devoted to his interview with Gartner he used the word "cut" eleven times. He used "saw" twice and "mutilate" three times as synonyms for cutting. He mentioned feeding tubes six times.[45]

Clearly, as Latimer had said in his confession, his immediate motive for the murder was the surgery, not disabilities as such although they played a large indirect role—he probably would never have considered murder as a method of helping any of his able-bodied children avoid surgery. Judging by his greater emphasis on the horror of feeding tubes, he was more terrified that Tracy would come home with such a tube than he was of any pain she would have had to endure. But Gartner didn't pick up on his phobic reaction to her questions. Gartner prepared for the interview with the help of a team of CBC producers and researchers. The result was that her interview did nothing to seriously challenge the media's line on the Latimer case. The way the media had chosen to tell the story had gained momentum, and was now unstoppable.

Finally, when the public formed opinions based on this one-sided picture, journalists incorporated those opinions into the story line that had been established. A week after Gartner's sympathetic interview with the Latimers she said the show had garnered an unprecedented number of responses, most supporting Latimer.[46]

All journalists should have asked how many other people would be jeopardized if the yardstick determining their eligibility for life rested on their ability to walk, talk or feed themselves. Stephen Hawking would fail that test. Many people in hospitals, nursing homes or their own homes cannot feed themselves. And what good is talking if no one will listen, as so often happens to disadvantaged people—as happened here?

Improvements

In the second trial some media approaches improved. The *Star Phoenix* included more disabled people as sources. David Roberts, the prairie bureau chief for the *Globe and Mail* who covered the second trial but not the first, included details omitted elsewhere. His sources and structure were more balanced.

Another positive signal came when the 1998 appeal verdict was about to be announced. CBC radio's morning national news on November 23, 1998 began to get it right. It did not describe Tracy as disabled until the second sentence and then only that she had a severe form of cerebral palsy. It even used a disabled source before turning to Mark Brayford.[47] However, the final summary reverted to the severely-disabled line and the CBC Winnipeg news broadcast later that morning gave the verdict entirely from the old perspective - as bad news for Robert Latimer.

CTV's *Canada AM* news on the same day stubbornly continued to call Tracy severely disabled and presented the case as a mercy killing. They did not even mention disabled people; it was all about Latimer's point of view.[48]

Later that day the local Winnipeg TV news on both networks was business as usual. CBC TV's Ross Rutherford again said Tracy couldn't walk, talk or feed herself and University of Manitoba law professor Barney Sneiderman advocated a third degree of homicide which he admitted would be used primarily when the victims are disabled. Yet both denied that the case was about disability and Sneiderman pointed to Justice Noble's statement that the case concerned pain, not disability.[49]

However, the changes were too little, too late. By this time the story was set; public opinion was firmly entrenched. Despite the *Star Phoenix's* attempts to provide better reporting of the second trial, one editorial showed how unyielding the attitudes of that publication's editorial writers were. They still regarded disabled critics as misguided interlopers, misdirecting the enlightened discussion on justice for compassionate killers. On December 2, 1997, the day after Noble announced the constitutional exemption, the editorial said:

> Much as it would serve justice for Latimer to let the case now rest, the Crown is likely to appeal the decision all the way to the Supreme Court—and not in the least because advocacy groups for the disabled have made it a case about their rights. Despite all evidence to the contrary, they remain convinced that Tracy Latimer's disability was the basis for her father's action. They refuse to acknowledge that this was a case about a loving father who couldn't bear to see his daughter suffer in unrelieved pain as she was subjected to ever intrusive medical procedures, including a plan to cut off the top of her thigh bones to disconnect them from her hips. And they wrongly want to make an example of him.[50]

The editorial demonstrates that its writers didn't connect their newspaper's constant references to Tracy's disabilities with the disability issues inherent in the case. They didn't realize that their publication along with many others had portrayed this as a disability-related mercy killing by connecting Latimer with euthanasia and the negative aspects of disability long before he stood in a courtroom. And they had made the link without evidence to support it.

What Should Have Been

Rules, whether from style books or minority groups, do not on their own provide enough guidance for stories like this one. Simplistic rules are never a substitute for sound judgement based on knowledge, experience and an open-minded, respectful attitude. That the reporters did not show such an attitude indicates a prevailing bias against disabled people.

It is true that, when speaking about disabled people or members of other visible minorities, the writer should avoid emphasizing features setting the subject apart from mainstream society. Disabled people have set their own rather rigid standards such as the phrase "persons with disabilities." They eschew "disabled people." Although this phrase can serve a useful function in names and slogans, it is too awkward and restrictive for most ordinary prose. Sometimes it defeats its purpose of emphasizing the person, not the disability. People remember beginnings and endings more easily than middles so the context of the phrase will determine whether "person" or "disability" is most prominent. If the phrase occurs at the beginning of a sentence, paragraph, etc., it will be more memorable than "disability." However, if it occurs at the end, "disability" will be more prominent. Instead, for the sake of flexibility, this book reserves this phrase for emphasis and variety but as a rule uses "disabled person" where "person" is the noun and "disabled" is an adjective subordinate to the noun.

Most writers still ignore even the simplest of guidelines. They avoid both preferred phrases and opt for an article in front of the adjective "disabled," making it into a noun and removing the person from the human race. Many use "disabled" and "handicapped" synonymously while a few still use "cripple."

Many are oblivious to the huge change in meaning one little preposition can make and consistently use "for" rather than "of" in names of disability rights organizations. The Council of Canadians with Disabilities often becomes the Council for Canadians with Disabilities, obliterating the group's self-advocacy mandate.

However, subjects like the Latimer case need thought and analysis, not just rules. Before even mentioning disability, the writer should determine whether it is relevant to the story and if so, how and where. Using the preferred phrase to describe Tracy or disabled observers would not have made a difference in the Latimer coverage where sources, structure and other elements said that disability is an undesirable feature overshadowing all others and that people with disabilities are not worthy of the same justice as able-bodied citizens; nor are they worthy to be experts on their own lives.

While Tracy's disabilities were relevant to the story, they did not apply everywhere. Consistently describing her only in those terms resulted in a portrayal of Tracy as nothing more than the sum of her disabilities and discomfort. It was perpetuating the negative bias.

Balance and fairness are as important in stories about disabled people as on any other subject. They involve identifying the principle characters and angles, ensuring that all receive equal, fair emphasis. In court it was Tracy versus her father and balanced coverage would have dispassionately presented the relevant facts about both.

A balanced view of Tracy's life would have included her good days as well as her bad. Presenting only her physical and mental abnormalities, her inability to speak and her supposed agony, did not allow readers to see her as a complete human being and assess for themselves the truthfulness of the defence arguments.

A more objective approach would have asked how the case would have been different if the victim had not been disabled—not only whether but how her disabilities were relevant to a story about her murder. In court her disabilities were being used to establish her suffering and provide the accused with a compassionate motive. Yet because disability in itself is not evidence of pain or suffering, the motive should have been connected only to evidence of Tracy's pain and the discrepancies in the argument should have been pointed out. It was the pain Latimer claimed to be ending. Cerebral palsy caused her disabilities which caused her pain. While these three could not be separated, they were also not synonymous.

An objective approach would also have been more cautious in using a disability descriptor. It was necessary to mention Tracy's physical and mental limitations only when referring to the attempted establishment of a compassionate motive and the necessity defence. It was not legitimate to describe Tracy's disabilities every time she was mentioned; nor was it accurate to talk only about the negative aspects of her life. Clearly her disabilities did not render her entire life unbearable.

Only with these questions answered would it have been appropriate to determine what the descriptor should be. In references to the victim outside the defence there should have been other descriptors balancing the defence line. Mark Brayford's attempts to dissociate Tracy's disabilities from her pain while using her dependency—that is, her disabilities—to support his arguments should have been exposed as the legal smokescreen they were.

Phrases like "couldn't walk, talk or feed herself" were misleading and largely irrelevant when the defence was arguing necessity. They may have applied when Gibbons was Latimer's lawyer and was talking about the burden of her care, but Latimer himself never claimed burden as his motive.

The right sources are also vital. Sports writers don't consult only hockey players' doctors and their parents about how the players experience the game or the resulting pain and injury. They ask the players. The same rule should apply when the subject is disability or pain resulting from disability.

Since the issue was ostensibly pain resulting from cerebral palsy and since pain is a subjective evaluation, journalists should have consulted, not care-givers, but the people at the heart of the issue—disabled people, preferably those who have had the surgery Latimer found so abhorrent. Only had the defence been burden would it have been legitimate to consult care-givers.

Reporters should have clarified the difference between necessity and mercy killing. The defence argument that Tracy's pain was unrelenting and that Latimer had no option but to kill her should have brought a barrage of questions and investigation into the validity of such an extreme statement. Journalists should have hammered at the doors of the developmental centre, the group home and the church to find out whether Tracy was always crying out in pain and, if so, why was she riding a school bus daily from the age of four until at least a week after her father had decided to kill her. They should have known from their experiences covering other trials that a truly objective account does not listen to the defence alone.

More importantly, they should have asked whether any level of pain should be admissible in court as a defence for murder. If it becomes a defence for Robert Latimer, how many people will hesitate to express their pain or ask for help fearing a death sentence instead of help?

Above all, they should have asked whether this was truly a mercy killing or a suicide, as the defendant protested. The evidence did not support comparing Tracy Latimer with Sue Rodriguez or making the Latimer case a part of the assisted suicide/euthanasia debate. Assisted suicide and euthanasia should have been included in the coverage only as part of Robert Latimer's defence.

The fact that this murder was placed in the euthanasia debate with only the victim's disabilities for evidence, as shown by the number of Latimer stories appearing in the *Canadian Index* euthanasia listing, shows how dangerous the legalization of these proposed end-of-life alternatives would be for all disabled citizens. This murder masquerading as mercy killing, even in the media coverage, is evidence of the prevailing negative bias against disability. In such a hostile atmosphere it would be impossible for disabled people's end-of-life choices to be honoured equally with their able-bodied counterparts.

The media cannot hide the crude bias of their approach to the Latimer case. The media have not been passive, objective observers of the Latimer case. They must accept their share of responsibility for the Canadian public's misperceptions of Tracy Latimer and her death.

Notes

1. Brent Jang - Canadian Press (November 7, 1994). "Farmer on trial in disabled daughter's killing." Halifax *Chronicle Herald*, A6.
2. Sheldon Smart (November 19, 1994). "Way media describe disabled in Latimer case said worrisome." Saskatoon *Star Phoenix*, A8.
3. Terry Craig (November 5, 1993). "Man accused of murdering daughter to appear in court." Saskatoon *Star Phoenix*, A3.
4. Regina *Leader Post* (November 10, 1993). "Wilkie man's bail hearing adjourned," A10.
5. Donella Hoffman (November 12, 1993.) "Man charged with daughter's murder not monster, not martyr, says lawyer." Saskatoon *Star Phoenix*, A3.
6. Bonny Braden (November 24, 1993). "Wilkie man changes lawyer." Saskatoon *Star Phoenix,* A6.
7. Beatrice A. Wright, "Attitudes and the Fundamental Bias," p. 19.
8. Brent Jang - Canadian Press (November 17, 1994). "Dad found guilty of killing daughter." Halifax *Chronicle Herald*, B6.
9. Brent Jang - Canadian Press (November 16, 1994). "Father had no choice but to kill girl: lawyer." Montreal *Gazette*, B1.
10. Canadian Press (November 8, 1894). "Farmer accused of killing his disabled daughter." *Globe and Mail*, A11.
11. Canadian Press (November 15, 1994). "Mother describes disabled girl's life: 'Her birth was way sadder than her death' court told of CP victim." The *Globe and Mail*, A3.
12. Brent Jang - Canadian Press (November 10, 1994). "'My priority was to put her out of pain,' sobbing father said." Montreal *Gazette,* B1.
13. Warren Goulding (November 15, 1994). "Death ended pain, mom says." Saskatoon *Star Phoenix*, A1.
14. Alanna Mitchell (November 10, 1994). "Palsy victims can live into 30s, doctor testifies." *Globe and Mail,* A10.
15. Brent Jang - Canadian Press (November 16, 1994). "Father had no choice but to kill girl: lawyer." Montreal *Gazette*, B1.
16. Warren Goulding (November 10, 1994). "Latimer confessed, say police." Saskatoon *Star Phoenix*, A3.
17. Alanna Mitchell (November 18, 1994). "Murder sentence stirs angry waves across the nation: Farmer may have been penalized for being too honest, professor says." *Globe and Mail*, A8.
18. Canadian Press (December 5, 1994). "'Revoke killer's sentence' Civil Liberties Association wants Latimer released." Calgary *Herald,* A3.
19. Canadian Press (November 18, 1994). "Others turn to Latimers for advice." Saskatoon *Star Phoenix*, B8.
20. Larry Johnsrude – Canadian Press (November 18, 1994). "Justice system lacks compassion for Latimer." Saskatoon *Star Phoenix*, C11.
21. Brent Jang - Canadian Press (November 30, 1994). "Latimer copes with

publicity." Halifax *Chronicle Herald*, A13.

22. Douglas Todd (December 19, 1994). "(The Tracy Latimer case) Father's 'tragic conundrum.'" Vancouver *Sun*, B3.

23. Montreal *Gazette* (November 18, 1994). "Mercy killing is murder: Law should not change because of exceptional case." B2.

24. Peggy (November 19, 1994). "A simple test : What if Tracy Latimer had been a healthy girl?" The Montreal *Gazette*, A3.

25. Canadian Press (December 24, 1994). "Sympathy growing for Latimer family." Calgary *Herald*, A25.

26. Sheldon Smart (November 19, 1994). "Way media describe disabled in Latimer case said worrisome." Saskatoon *Star Phoenix*, A8.

27. CBC TV (November 25, 1997). *The National Magazine*.

28. CBC TV (December 1, 1997). *The National Magazine*.

29. Alanna Mitchell (November 10, 1994). "Palsy victims can live into 30s, doctor testifies." *Globe and Mail*, A10.

30. Brent Jang - Canadian Press (November 9, 1994). "Child needed constant care." Calgary *Herald*, A12.

31. Brent Jang - Canadian Press (November 9, 1994). "Child needed constant care." Calgary *Herald*, A12.

32. Warren Goulding (November 9, 1994). "Officer suspicious from start," Saskatoon *Star Phoenix*, A3.

33. Warren Goulding, (November 10, 1994) "Latimer confessed, say police," Saskatoon *Star Phoenix*, A3.

34. Canadian Press (November 15, 1994). "Mother describes disabled girl's life: 'Her birth was way sadder than her death,' court told of CP victim," *Globe and Mail*, A3.

35. Brent Jang - Canadian Press (November 10, 1994). "'My priority was to put her out of pain,' sobbing father said." Montreal *Gazette*, B1.

36. Brent Jang - Canadian Press (November 17, 1994). "Dad found guilty of killing daughter." Halifax *Chronicle Herald*, B6.

37. Brent Jang - Canadian Press (November 17, 1994). "Father who killed disabled daughter jailed, can't get parole for 10 years." Vancouver *Sun*, A1.

38. Warren Goulding (November 17, 1994). "Latimer Guilty," Saskatoon *Star Phoenix*, A1.

39. Brent Jang - Canadian Press (November 17, 1994). "Dad found guilty of killing daughter." Halifax *Chronicle Herald*, B6.

40. Brent Jang - Canadian Press (November 17, 1994). "Dad found guilty of killing daughter." Halifax *Chronicle Herald*, B6.

41. Warren Goulding (November 16, 1994). "Latimer's fate in hands of jury." Saskatoon *Star Phoenix*, A1, A6.

42. Canadian Press (November 16, 1994). "Dad forced to kill disabled daughter—defence." Halifax *Chronicle Herald*, A16.

43. Art Robinson (November 18, 1994). "Support pouring in for Latimer family." Saskatoon *Star Phoenix*, A1, B8.

44. Sharon Doyle Driedger (November 17, 1997). "Should Latimer go free?" *Maclean's*, 12-14.

45. CBC TV (November 25, 1997). *The National Magazine*.

46. CBC TV (December 1, 1997). *The National Magazine.*
47. CBC Radio One (November 23, 1998). *National News.*
48. CTV (November 23, 1998). *Canada AM News.*
49. CBC Radio (November 23, 1998). *Winnipeg News.*
50. Saskatoon *Star Phoenix* (December 2, 1997). "Latimer case far from over." A4.

Chapter Three

Coming Out of the Attic:
A Brief History
of Disabled People's Activism

The legal and media handling of the Latimer case and the outpouring of public support for Latimer left the disabled community stunned and bewildered. For decades they had demonstrated that disability, pain, suffering, and what the Latimers called "mutilation" were not the end of life nor even the "quality of life," however that well-worn phrase may be defined. Yet here were the age-old prejudices again. Latimer's defence and the media denied the importance of disability even while they used Tracy's disabilities to make her father's actions look like mercy killing. It was as though a quarter century of disability activism hadn't happened.

Disabled activists across Canada and around the world have exorcised a number of the demons that had isolated them and made them feel like a collection of defective body parts, less than fully human. Some had left their sense of inferiority behind and come to feel equal to able-bodied Canadians.

Their struggle for equality opposed negative images of them painted by charities, institutions, the medical and rehabilitation systems and by eugenics programs. But the most insidious demons were the ones they carried inside. Like abuse victims, many still keenly felt the stigma imposed on them by dominant able-bodied views. They felt inferior.

They know their experiences are often misinterpreted even by experts such as those called by Latimer's defence attorney. While experts may have superior knowledge and training, their attitudes and values are not necessarily different than those of other Canadians. In addition to projecting their own discomfort with disability onto the disabled person, the attitudes of many professionals and leaders are also still rooted in the hierarchical medical and rehabilitation systems, the degrading sentiments and practices of charitable systems and in the overt prejudice of eugenics.

A Deadly Pecking Order

When seven-year-old Mel Graham left his home in Regina, Saskatch-ewan to attend the Brantford School for the Blind in Ontario his life was already a considerable improvement over that of disabled people in preceding centuries. In the mid-1950s children from all over Canada were assembled into that school. "That was the standard prescription," he says. And, although he had 5 percent vision, he went there as well.

As difficult as it was for such a young boy to go so far away from home to unlock the wonders of Braille and learn about the world, it was not nearly as difficult as his life would have been a century or two earlier. Before Louis Braille developed his touch-based system of read-ing and writing in the mid-nineteenth century, blind people and those with other disabilities had few options. Either their families maintained them, often hiding them in attics, or they were thrust onto whatever public support system there was.[1]

In Victorian England that system was the infamous poorhouses immortalized by Charles Dickens. Those places, which were deliber-ately made as miserable as possible, segregated the sexes—even married couples—to prevent the poor from producing more undesira-bles. The disabled people of the time were not tracked as a separate group but most were likely among the poor.

The poorhouses resulted from the 1834 New Poor Law based on economic theories developed at the turn of the nineteenth century by Thomas Robert Malthus. He said poverty was unavoidable because the number of poor always would outstrip food production and only war, famine and disease could check population growth; later he added moral restraint. Charles Darwin's theory of the evolution of species has roots in Malthusianism.

Darwin's cousin, Sir Francis Galton, picked up the thread taking it a step further. He discovered the inheritance factor in intelligence and, based on that limited knowledge, developed the notion of eugenics which said the quality of the human race could be improved by selec-tively breeding out genetically weak traits. In this belief, eugenics steps away from the supposed neutrality of science and places genetics within a value system. It automatically dehumanizes some people by dividing humanity into perceived positive and negative genetic attributes and devaluing those with the so-called negative traits.

The Victorian eugenics movement soon spread to Europe and North America where it took on a variety of shapes. Sweden, Canada and the United States preferred to control reproduction of undesirables through sterilization. While Victorian England may have developed these ideas in the nineteenth century, the practice of eliminating the weak and outcasts is as old as superstition; in ancient Greece the Spartans and

72

others got rid of disabled children by leaving them to die of exposure, while sick people were allowed to commit suicide by drinking hemlock. A Canadian Medical Association publication says: "Some authors believe that it was a reaction against the increasing frequency of this practice, including the administration of poison, that led to the Hippocratic Oath."[2] China has been using a related technique since 1994, restricting marriages of persons with certain disabilities and diseases.

In Canada's twentieth-century eugenics program, the sterilization was supposed to have safeguards such as more than one expert opinion plus informed consent, but the Alberta program illustrated how feeble those safeguards were. The Alberta Provincial Training School for Mental Defectives sterilized more than 4,700 residents between 1923 and 1972, most without a second opinion and certainly without informed consent. Most of the residents didn't even fall within the institution's own definition of mental defective or have the genetic disorders at which the eugenics program was aimed. Evidence also points to native people and members of ethnic minorities being targeted for forced sterilization more than other groups.[3]

Even by the time this program began, the study of genetics was disproving the foundation on which eugenics rested. Many disorders presumed to be genetically based had other causes such as disease or malnutrition. In fact most disabilities are not genetic in origin. They are the result of wars, accidents, illnesses or medical and scientific interventions, malfunctions or outright bungling. Thalidomide survivors are a testament to a medication gone wrong and Laura Latimer thought the brain damage leading to Tracy's cerebral palsy resulted from the attending staff's inability to recognize the baby's distress during labour because of a broken fetal heart monitor. However, in the 1920s and 1930s, public opinion and the politics of the day blindly carried the Alberta program forward.

In Germany the Nazis picked up the eugenics banner with a vengeance, at first sterilizing 300,000 disabled people, then turning to extermination. They killed an estimated 70,000 disabled people, perhaps as many as 275,000, and the methods used became the blueprint for what the Third Reich called the final solution against the Jews.[4] A memorial has been erected to these forgotten victims in Hadamar's clinic, now a psychiatric hospital. It was one of six clinics where German doctors sent patients with disabilities ranging from spina bifida to depression. In Hadamar a band once played to celebrate the killing of the clinic's 10,000[th] victim.[5]

When the Holocaust atrocities against the Jews were discovered by the Allied countries, the first reaction of the victorious side was disbelief, then horror and revulsion, but they aimed that revulsion at the

Nazi regime, not at the underlying cause. The Nazi euthanasia program against disabled people is still largely unknown.

In Canada, the public response to the Latimer case sends a shiver of fear through the disabled community because it is frighteningly similar to the case in Nazi Germany that sparked the extermination there. Early in 1939 a man with a severely disabled son asked Hitler for permission to end his child's life. Hitler sent his personal physician, Karl Brandt, to assess the situation. Upon the doctor's confirmation of the father's story the boy was killed.

Other cases soon followed and the number of victims rapidly multiplied. Dick Sobsey of the University of Alberta Abuse and Disability Project wrote that safeguards were used. In each case two physicians had to confirm that these people were incurable and their lives were not worth living. Before carbon monoxide canisters were used, exhaust fumes were the preferred method of extermination. "Later, custom built gas chambers were built . . . To prevent the victims from being alarmed, the gas chambers were disguised as shower rooms." This method was later used in the infamous concentration camps.[6]

Disabled people know that suffering cannot be eliminated by eliminating the sufferers or disability by eradicating disabled people. Because disability can occur at any time in life, mercy killing would eventually touch the majority as it did in Nazi Germany. Because disability is frequently confused with suffering—as it was in the Latimer case—this thinking is extremely dangerous.

It is a shameful fact that Canada shared the way of thinking that led to the holocaust in Germany. Canada stripped vulnerable citizens of basic human rights, and had other dehumanizing, destructive values and practices.

Charity

Charity has at least as long a history as the attitudes behind eugenics and has attracted many genuinely altruistic people. On the one hand it has deep roots in love of and concern for one's less fortunate fellow human beings but on the other it can have quite a nasty streak. The former empowers the receiver as well as the giver, while the negative types of charity are just as steeped in control over the recipient as is outright hatred.

When dealing with the topic of disability the positive side is obvious and doesn't need to be belaboured here; charities have done much to improve the physical conditions of disabled people. But the other side of good deeds is rarely if ever acknowledged. Gifts are automatically assumed to be altruistic.

Publicly flaunted charity usually divides society into the fortunate givers and the unfortunate receivers. In Charles Dickens' A Christmas Carol the wealthy Ebenezer Scrooge demonstrates his change of heart by giving to the poor. His money also gives Tiny Tim access to a cure for his disability. While Tiny Tim has become an enduring icon of disability, his role in the story is brief, restricted to looking pathetically grateful in contrast to his benefactor's generosity. While Scrooge's gifts in themselves are laudable, much of his altruism is public and there is no talk of equality between Scrooge and the recipients of his charity. This story, one which is still popular more than 150 years after Dickens wrote it, illustrates the deep roots and contradictions of the charity ethic.

In contrasting giver and receiver, charity participates in making social outcasts of the recipients, in dehumanizing them. While in some places disabilities are seen as divine retribution for the person's sins or the sins of the parents, charitable gifts are evidence of the giver's superior moral standards. In the late 1800s homes and hospitals for incurables and lunatic asylums, as they were called at the time, were monuments to the charitable motives and wealth of those who sponsored them.[7]

For thousands of years disabled people throughout the world were relegated to the fringes of their communities, surviving on other people's leftovers and the occasional meager monetary handout. Usually isolated or part of a tiny minority segregated by immense physical barriers and the rejection of the majority, they were reduced to begging, or panhandling as we now call it, and in many places their situation has not changed.

Taking care of unfortunates by giving them the necessities of life has been associated historically with religion but charity eventually became entwined with more secular institutions as well. It also became more organized. Canadian hospitals, agencies and other institutions now use sophisticated charitable appeals to raise operating money.

The problems arising for disabled people from charity were not a result of the gifts themselves but of the accompanying attitudes of the givers and the charitable organizations. The strings attached to the gifts robbed the receivers of their autonomy. Decision-making, even on personal matters, was taken from the recipients and handed to the givers.

The many rehabilitation agencies which sprang up after World War II relied to a large extent on private charity and were developed around these attitudes. Some were created by charitable organizations such as the Kinsmen. With the aid of newer communications technology those sentiments translated into fund-raising efforts like telethons dripping with pity. Advertisements sharply contrasted the powerlessness of the lowly recipients with the powerful, philanthropic donors and widened the social gap between them.[8] Even now one sees the occasional commercial still using this technique: a disadvantaged person silently offering a pathetic contrast with the good-looking, well-dressed personality pontificating about the sufferer's plight, then pleading for donations.

In the eyes of disabled activists, these telethons and similar charitable fund-raising did more harm than good for the clients' public image and self esteem.[9] Portraying disabled people's lives as perpetually tragic fed the fear of disability and increased the tendency to associate disability with disease and even death. It should be no surprise that viewers accustomed to such images shunned disabled people and relegated them to segregated schools, housing and special programs and treated them as social pariahs.

The association with death is evident in the similarity of the shunning experienced by both disabled and dying people. Anne Mullens, author of *Timely Death*, wrote, "Family, friends and strangers may even begin to treat the sick individual as delicate or powerless, talking to the patient like a child or as if he or she weren't there, even if the patient's mental faculties are entirely intact."[10] This passage could have been about disabled people instead of terminally ill patients.

In this way charity kept disabled people out of sight and out of mind just as effectively as institutionalization. The form of giving charity had evolved but the attitudes hadn't. Many of these methods began to change when disabled people criticized the old style and themselves became involved in charitable fund-raising as one method of getting funds for their own organizations, such as the "Come Fly with Us" kite festival of the Winnipeg Independent Living Resource Centre. The Winnipeg Children's Hospital Research Foundation's annual Teddy Bear Picnic taps into children's healthy ability to adapt to illness and disability through play. Habitat for Humanity insists on "sweat equity" from the recipient and a partnership between giver and receiver.

Institutions

In western countries the nineteenth century also saw the institutionalism of disabled people who were placed in impersonal warehouses that had some advantages over life on the street but, even at their best, were not homes.

Abuse of and experimentation on the residents was not uncommon. In the twentieth century Dr. Ewen Cameron's brainwashing experiments in Montreal, sponsored by the United States Central Intelligence Agency, robbed his mental patients of their memories, sometimes even their personalities. Some of the involuntary sterilization performed at the Alberta Training School for Mental Defectives was on already sterile boys and was done for experimentation purposes, not for the institution's stated intention of preventing reproduction.

For the residents, institutions tended to foster a mindset that precluded them from seeking independence. "It either broke you or it made you," Mel Graham says. A few graduates of the Brantford school became great achievers but most became under-achievers working at low-expectation jobs in broom factories or CNIB canteens. "It breeds a homogeneous kind of product," Graham says.

In these institutions, administrators and staff set the rules and in return expected compliance and docility from the residents whom they viewed as incapable of running their own lives. To a large extent institutionalization still produces such docility. Patients who have been shut away from their communities for a long time feel uncertainty and fear when they are released. Either they or their outside circumstances have changed and suddenly they have no one to dictate the appropriate response.

Life within large institutions is not determined solely by staff members. Most institutional personnel are caring people but, particularly in large facilities, circumstances will always tend to dictate that autonomy and personal responsibility, the citizenship rights of those for whom the institution was created, are absent. Smaller institutions like group homes can be more like a real home, with meaningful input from the residents.

Children are especially susceptible to the negative effects of the impersonal institutionalization characteristic of large facilities. When four-year-old Pat Danforth, then of Victoria, was hospitalized for months in 1953 after getting her right hand caught in a wringer washer, patients were allowed visitors only on Wednesday afternoons. Patients were kept in hospitals much longer than now. Consequently only her mother and not her naval officer father could see her. "We lived for Wednesday afternoons," she said. Pat said she became quite attached to some of the staff and doctors as though they had become her surrogate family. The institutionalization bred a fear of rejection that haunted her into her adult years and destroyed her marriage.

Children housed in medical and rehabilitation institutions also picked up the medical language and attitudes toward their conditions. Many learned to name themselves as "paraplegics" or "quadriplegics" or the abbreviated forms, "paras" and "quads." Patients' names became secondary to their room and bed numbers.

Small wonder that Ulrich (Rick) Woelcke, a retired social worker with the Society for Manitobans with Disabilities, with whom I've had many conversations, noticed in the 1960s that people who became disabled early in life took less initiative in the rehabilitation process than those whose disabilities occurred later. They had been largely molded into a passive existence. To them making their own decisions and taking on responsibilities was part of the frightening unknown.

Some institutions like hospitals may always be necessary, particularly for short-term acute medical care. For those with disorders like Alzheimer Disease nursing homes may be the best option, but many, who in past years would have been locked into nursing homes, now continue to live at home with the help of home care. In some apartment complexes, residents share meal and housekeeping services while retaining independent living quarters.

For some like Tracy Latimer, permanent institutionalization may still be the only viable alternative to home. However, according to CCD coordinator Laurie Beachell, the disabled community prefers smaller more home-like settings such as group homes with emphasis on resident autonomy. One cooperative model, the Qu'Appelle Project, is described in Chapter Four.

The Western Medical and Rehabilitation Systems

The western medical and rehabilitation systems were also major influences in the lives of disabled people. While they improved physical care for patients, these systems fell seriously short of truly recognizing the humanity of the people receiving that care.

The medical system treats sick "patients," as it labels care recipients. It has the physician at its head with other staff answering to him/her. Sick persons seek the advice of the doctor or expert and then follow that advice. Illnesses requiring admission to the system's institutions require that patients step out of their customary places in the home and community, away from their responsibilities temporarily. Patients who resist the control of the system, challenge the doctor's authority or in some way do not fall into the role set out for them, are often viewed as troublemakers.

Medical terminology dehumanizes when it treats patients' names as secondary to their conditions or disabilities for identification purposes: Jane Doe with two paralyzed limbs becomes a paraplegic, John Brown with four limb involvement is a quadriplegic; Sam Small with hemophilia is labeled a hemophiliac. Dehumanization makes it easier for those with decision-making power to avoid consulting those without that power, the patients.

Rehabilitation was an outgrowth of the western medical model. It adopted medical terminology and, like medicine, treated disabled people as sick except that these patients would never get well. Some able-bodied people confused this permanence with terminal illness as seemed to occur in the Latimer case: Justice Ted Noble and many observers compared Tracy's situation with that of terminally ill adults even though cerebral palsy is not a terminal illness and Tracy's weight problem was likely compounded by her parents' refusal of a feeding tube.

Early rehabilitation gave the clients, as they came to be called, the same exemptions as medical patients, only here the exemptions were permanent. This rehabilitation excused disabled people from employment and responsibilities entirely. It expected them to spend the rest of their lives like children, occupying their waking hours in leisure activities protected by their able-bodied care-givers, sheltered from the dangers of taking risks. And the outside world saw these segregated people as pathetic "others."

Wars and particularly World War II and the years following it were major turning points in medicine and rehabilitation. In 1854 Florence Nightingale created the nursing profession when she recruited thirty-eight women to attend to the wounded on the battlefields of the Crimean War. The late nineteenth and early twentieth centuries brought new industries and other professions aimed at recovery and rehabilitation. During the last half of World War II the mass production of penicillin, discovered in 1928 by the Scottish bacteriologist Sir Alexander Fleming, saved the lives of countless injured soldiers. Each discovery or innovation not only saved lives but also increased the number of disabled soldiers surviving their injuries.[11]

While these advances saved lives and increased the mobility of disabled people, their purpose did not include disabled people becoming decision makers about their own lives.[12] In the optimistic post-World War II period, medical and rehabilitation professionals began to see disabilities as surmountable to some extent, providing of course, that disabled people still followed orders from the increasing numbers of experts studying what was viewed as the patients' or clients' problems. These social workers, physical therapists and occupational therapists, to name only a few, judged the success of the rehabilitation on how well the clients followed prescriptions. Failure meant the clients had failed.

Rick Woelcke told me that when he became a social worker with Winnipeg's Society for Crippled Children and Adults in 1959, the prevailing attitude in his field said rehabilitation was uncertain for clients who were railing against their circumstances, not "accepting" their disabilities.

Clearly the clients were supposed to accept their new social position, the prescribed subservience and the advice of the agency experts. Their resistance made many professionals feel uncomfortable. Allen Simpson said his questions ruffled a few feathers. At age fifteen he was being encouraged by his doctor to use braces to improve circulation. "I remember being picked up by a Cadillac and driven to the Anderson's House of Orthopedics." When he asked why his doctor and the owner of Anderson's were always together when he was being assessed, he found a finger in his face punctuating stern orders not to say such things again.

While some professionals grew in their awareness and understanding, rehabilitation agencies were still organized to run disabled peoples' lives for them from the onset of the disability to the grave. They, not their clients, set goals based on the assessed degree of disability and then, based on that assessment, placed less-disabled clients on an employment track while those deemed unemployable were put on what they called the independent living track. Unlike current definitions used by the disabled community, independent living was seen by the rehabilitation system as an alternative to full integration, not a part of it. It did not consider full, equal participation in the community a realistic goal for the clients.

Young war veterans were not content to be restricted by these attitudes, charitable fund-raising and segregating special programs. They had experienced real adult life and weren't about to give it up. Because they had acquired their disabilities in the defence of their country, the public was more accepting of them than of other disabled people.

However, some young survivors of diseases and other disabling circumstances were not content with the status quo either. Their appetite for full integration had been whetted by the same rehabilitation that was now holding them back. The tantalizing carrot of full equality and participation was being dangled just out of reach.

Many knew they could handle much more than the facade of independence being offered to them. The schooling they received rarely led to university or employment. Often the emphasis of programs, especially for those labeled severely disabled, was passive leisure and entertainment.

But what good was education without meaningful employment or activities in which to use that learning? How could they engage in such employment or activities without access to affordable public transportation? How could they relate to able-bodied co-workers or friends or how could those people ever see them as equals if they couldn't socialize in integrated settings? How could they ever be taken seriously if they were perpetual dependants, never making their own decisions? Not a great prospect for anyone, but particularly not for young disabled people to whom such a life stretched before them like a desert without an oasis.

In the initial stages of the self-advocacy movement, agencies were one of the primary targets as disabled people became their own experts, wresting control of their lives from able-bodied professionals. As with charity, their goal was not to end the services provided by medicine and rehabilitation or to refuse pain-relieving, beneficial medical intervention, but to take over the decision-making that rightfully belonged to them as adults and citizens. They wanted their life goals to be their own.

Advocacy for Disabled People

The nineteenth century also gave birth to the first advocacy groups. However, like institutions, these advocacy groups were generally rooted in and funded by charity. They were formed by able-bodied people for disabled people, at first for deaf and blind children and later for other types of disability.

With the development of Braille blind people could become literate. It is still used today although computers are playing a greater role in deciphering the printed word. Since Braille showed that one sense can, to some extent, compensate for the loss of another, it is no wonder that sensory disabilities were the first to be addressed.

Although these organizations were paternalistic, they did set the stage for self-advocacy by demonstrating that speaking out could change things. It was still able-bodied people speaking on behalf of disabled dependents but at least the object was no longer to hide their disabilities.

The assumption was still that disabled people could not speak for themselves and perhaps at that time they couldn't, not because of their inability to voice their needs but because no one would listen to them without an able-bodied intermediary. They also hadn't yet discarded their own negative views of themselves and they hadn't acquired the leadership skills to take over.

Then, too, organizations have a habit of taking on lives of their own and their leaders then have vested interests in maintaining the status quo. So this type of advocacy could not and would not achieve true integration for the very people at which these advocacy efforts were targeted. To attain that goal the advocacy had to be by disabled people, not just for them.

Real Change—Self Awareness

The achievements of disability advocacy groups did not come gift wrapped. In order to achieve anything at all they had to break down a lot of barriers. They had to demolish their physical isolation, their shyness, their inexperience with leadership. They had to learn to work together without assistance from the organizations that had traditionally dominated, patronized and defined them.

They had to define themselves both as individuals and as a group.

Before they could do that they had to crawl out from under the oppressive attitudinal and physical weights that had burdened them, that they themselves had accepted as a fact of life in a vain attempt to fit into the culture around them.

To some of them, becoming part of a self-advocacy group was a liberating but frightening experience. They had not been in the habit of deciding when and what they would eat, never mind taking on the agencies and governments on which they relied. During the planning sessions of the steering committee to form the Manitoba League of the Physically Handicapped, now the Manitoba League of Persons with Disabilities, "some felt that social service organizations should be included because disabled people should be grateful for the services they had been given.... They felt that perhaps disabled people should not ask for too many more privileges in society."[13]

Clearly this segment of the disabled population did not separate rights from privileges. In their distorted self-image they were so inferior to the rest of the community that they didn't have the right to ask for services able-bodied people would consider necessities. They could not yet see that no able-bodied Canadian can get along without the support of the rest of the community; they think nothing of publicly funded services such as education to produce a more informed and literate citizenry and workforce. Somehow these budding advocates had been brainwashed into believing that these same services were not for them, that they should forever stand outside the warm embrace of their communities.

To other disabled people, becoming part of such a group felt like a step backward. They already had a fair degree of autonomy. They were educated, some had jobs or even careers. A group struggling to learn the basics of running meetings and offices was too confining. They saw themselves as superior to the less worldly members. However, despite some conflicts, the diverse members of the different groups did ultimately gel into a force out to change the world.

When the disability self-advocacy movement began, the lives of disabled people were still severely restricted. During the Manitoba steering committee meetings, "One blind fellow remembered when there were no services at all."[14]

Curbs prevented wheelchair users from travelling beyond the block where they had been deposited. They often had to enter public buildings by circuitous means such as loading docks or service elevators, if they could get in at all. Frequently steps barred them, requiring several muscular people to lift them, often endangering both them and the lifters. Washrooms and public transportation were inaccessible.

Work for people with severe physical, mental and intellectual disabilities was usually in sheltered workshops which were exempted from health and safety regulations, offered little meaningful employment and paid well below the minimum wage because the workers were perpetually in "training." As a result the workers were left dependent on the rehabilitation and public support systems for the necessities of life. This dependency in turn amputated their right to make decisions for themselves and lead an adult life.

The public treated them the way the medical rehabilitation system portrayed them: regardless of their age they were children and their activities were meaningless to able-bodied observers. The efforts of the disabled person would be greeted with great gasps of amazement and patronizing encouragement such as that given to children; if they fumbled or made a mistake, someone else would instantly take over.

Without protection from discrimination disabled people were unwelcome in most workplaces or could be evicted from a restaurant or bar simply because the disability disturbed another patron. Consequently the least threatening places for disabled people were their own homes. Because of these restrictions on their movement and access to the job market they overwhelmingly tended to be poor and those disabled early in life also tended to be under-educated, exacerbating the vicious cycle of poverty and dependence.

But not all homes were havens. Many parents, family members and other care-givers struggled with their own fears and misunderstandings about disability and acted on assumptions arising from their own feelings. Heselton said, "Sometimes the parents of disabled children can be the worst." By taking over not only all care of the child but also all decision making, such parents can create an acquired helplessness and increase the burden of caring for a disabled child.

Many also think that, if they themselves are suffering because of the disability, then their disabled child's suffering must be worse than their own. Their difficulties become the child's. Robert Latimer may well have projected his own fears onto Tracy. The second trial mentioned his extreme fear of needles and medical intervention causing tissue damage. His sister testified that he couldn't bear to look at so much as a picture of a syringe on the cover of a magazine. If he was that afraid of even the most ordinary of medical procedures, he must have been terrified of Tracy's upcoming surgery, not because of the pain it would cause her, but because of the pain it would cause him, although he may not have distinguished between the two.

Many other homes and parents were more supportive and encouraging as Heselton's were, and while she could step around the pervasive and invasive influence of medicine and rehabilitation, many disabled people couldn't.

A Voice Unheard

Then came the sixties and widespread public opposition in the United States to the bigotry and narrow-minded thinking that had kept under-valued people from attaining their potentials. African Americans and Vietnam war veterans demanded their civil rights. Ralph Nader's Raiders demonstrated the power of the ordinary consumer. Women asserted their right to equal opportunities.

In Canada as in the United States disabled people listened, watched, learned. And, led mostly by young mobility-impaired professionals and students, they learned how to leave their attics and the prisons of their stereotyped roles. They organized what author Diane Driedger called The Last Civil Rights Movement, the title of her book on the international disability advocacy organization, Disabled Peoples' International. Disabled people became aware of the oppression they had endured. They began to perceive themselves as a distinct group with distinct needs but the same rights as everyone else, rights they had not been exercising. And they began to behave as members of their own group.

Questioning the power the medical and rehabilitation systems had over them helped clarify their goals. They began to see themselves first and foremost as people whose lives mattered. They were not worthless throwaways. They were not helpless victims of disease or injury. They were not objects of charity whose lives had to be run by experts, whose smiles in the face of adversity inspired others, whose lack of ability made everybody else look good.

They learned to value themselves by standards other than high-ranking jobs or social positions. They were valuable because they had lives to live and, just like everyone else, they wanted to make what they could of their lives.

They chose to call themselves "consumers" in keeping with the consumer movement that had initially inspired them. They, too, were using services offered by providers of medical expertise, social services, rehabilitation techniques and other necessities. As consumers they had the right to influence the quality of those services.

They had to fight for their rights themselves because the method of attaining the goal was as important as the goal itself. The means coloured the end. To have the rehabilitation system fight for their independence was still dependency.[15] They would still be speaking through an interpreter with a vested interest in thwarting their goals. As Phil Fontaine, National Chief of the Assembly of First Nations has said, rights cannot be given; they have to be taken.

Disabled activists developed their own definition of independent living closer to that of the able-bodied population. To them it meant the opportunity to leave the sheltered environment of institutions or their parental homes, earn their own living, take risks, enjoy entertainment in public places, marry and have families. It meant using services such as home care in order to meet their goals.

And they rejected the standard definition of independence as doing everything without help. After all, what able-bodied person is totally self reliant? Doesn't everybody use motorized wheelchairs called cars dependent on publicly funded roads? Doesn't everyone enjoy other publicly funded services such as sidewalks or schools without relinquishing autonomy?

Organizing in Canada

Canadians with disabilities "have come a long way, baby" as the old cigarette slogan said, but they have a much longer way to go before they reach their goal of full physical and attitudinal accessibility. To them physical accessibility refers to the elimination of physical barriers while attitudinal accessibility comes when able-bodied people accept disabled people as full, equal citizens. Physical barriers fall when attitudes change. Mel Graham says, "We are in the business of changing the yardsticks by which disabled people are measured."

In Canada the seeds of this movement sprouted in the 1960s led by groups such as disabled athletes whose mobility had been increased by improvements in wheelchairs and prostheses. In Manitoba the Wheelchair Sports and Recreation Association turned to activism when it rallied American, Mexican, Argentinian and Jamaican wheelchair groups, successfully demonstrating to Pan American Games organizers to demand a parallel wheelchair event right after the 1967 games in Winnipeg. The association continued to meet monthly after the games and in time the conversations led from sports to the inaccessibility of public transportation and other obstacles they faced daily.

Laurie Beachell, coordinator of the Council of Canadians with Disabilities, said Marc Lalonde, then minister of Health and Welfare, fuelled this growing awareness in 1970 by suggesting that the proliferating agencies consult their clients before coming to him. Lalonde recognized that "handicapped people want out from under ... sheltered workshops, over-protective institutions segregated recreation, paternalism and tokenism." Beachell said the agencies were "an uncoordinated mess involving itself in policy ... an agency per disease per body part." He surmised that the starting point for discussion was recreation because it was less threatening to the agencies than issues like employment and education.

Allan Simpson, one of these first organizers, regarded recreation as a wonderful tool for demonstrating the capabilities of the athletes and changing public opinion about disability. To some countries like Mexico which don't get many medals abroad, wheelchair sports was an opportunity for international recognition they couldn't pass up. The incentive of medals led the Mexican government to support the development of other services their wheelchair athletes needed.

The Canadian Rehabilitation Council for the Disabled (CRCD), a national partnership of rehabilitation organizations, accepted Lalonde's challenge. Member provincial organizations each asked disabled clients to select six delegates for the November 1973 First National Rehabilitation Conference of the Physically Disabled in Toronto. However, the goal was to form an advisory committee, not to share power.

By this time provincial advocacy organizations had formed in Alberta and Saskatchewan. In 1972 two regional groups, one each from Edmonton and Lethbridge, formed the Alberta Committee of Action Groups for the Disabled incorporated in 1973, the same year as Saskatchewan's The Voice of the Handicapped.

Delegates to the rehabilitation conference returned more inspired by meeting each other than by the thought of belonging to CRCD's advisory committee and the six Manitoba delegates asked for advice from the Saskatchewan Voice on forming their own group. Their January 1974 meeting sparked the formation of the Manitoba League of the Physically Handicapped later that year.[16]

Next year Prince Edward Island followed suit. British Columbia incorporated in 1978 and the Nova Scotia League for Equal Opportunities in 1979. In Ontario the older United Handicapped Groups of Ontario stepped aside in 1981 to allow for the creation of Persons United for Self Help (PUSH) a more advocacy-oriented multi-disability organization.

By 1981 all provinces except New Brunswick and the territories had formal structures in place and those three areas still have none. Eventually all of the provincial groups expanded their vision to include all disabilities. PUSH collapsed in 1994, Beachell said, from internal and external pressures resulting from the unfulfilled election promises of the provincial NDP government

A National Voice

The provincial groups soon recognized the need for a national body through which they could jointly address public and private sector issues at the federal level. Working together would also increase their own credibility and strength.

Immediately after the Manitoba League of the Physically Handicapped was incorporated in 1975 it invited representatives from Alberta and Saskatchewan to its fall conference where informal discussions led to the creation in 1976 of the Coalition of Provincial Organizations of the Handicapped or COPOH, now the Council of Canadians with Disabilities or CCD. With its head office in Winnipeg, it now directly or indirectly includes more than 160 organizations representing several hundred thousand disabled Canadians.

CCD allows other national organizations on its board, but in order that they not outnumber the provincial groups who started the organization, their number must be one fewer than the number of provincial groups. They must be self-advocate bodies; parents advocating for children are not included. Therefore, although some disabled people are members of the Cerebral Palsy Association, this organization is not a member of CCD because it operates primarily from the parental perspective.

The national members that make up CCD are more limited in scope than the umbrella body, focussing on either a single disability or a single issue. CCD deals with the root causes of a problem such as the Employment Insurance training which, because it is limited to those on EI, excludes many disabled people who have problems getting, let alone losing, jobs.

CCD rejects the government's answer of creating a separate pot of money for disabled people, the very concept they have been fighting for the past twenty years. They want services provided by the same departments serving the general population. "All our work focuses on legislative framework for inclusion," Beachell said.

National Members of CCD

Following are some of the key member organizations of CCD.

DisAbled Women's Network of Canada (DAWN Canada). A national cross-disability organization of women with disabilities focussing on issues related to both disability and feminism. They work for inclusion in the women's movement, access to women's services, and on other issues such as violence, suicide, justice and policing. Not happy with being identified by the negative prefix "dis" they capitalized the "A" in their name to emphasize their abilities.

The Canadian Association of the Deaf. A self-advocacy affiliation of thirty local, provincial and regional organizations of Canada's estimated 260,000 profoundly deaf sign-language users. Its purpose is to promote and protect their rights, concerns and needs in such areas as education, interpreting and television access.

Thalidomide Victims Association of Canada (TVAC). Although TVAC has been incorporated since 1988, it wasn't until 1992 that it broke away from the War Amputations of Canada. It was the year the ninety-four members, representing 135 Canadian thalidomiders, as they call themselves, won compensation for their foreshortened limbs and other complications acquired before birth, when thalidomide was prescribed for their mothers' morning sickness. Their organization's goals have been expanded to address needs other than mere compensation.

National Educational Association of Disabled Students (NEADS). With a representative from each province and territory as well as member groups on nearly forty campuses, NEADS is a communication network for disabled college and university students. It collects and disseminates information on post-secondary education and the disabled student and promotes accessibility on all Canadian campuses.

The National Network for Mental Health. A provincial and territorial network of psychiatric survivors and consumers trying to improve the lives of Canadians using the mental health system. They admit to internal differences on mental illness, treatment and medication but are dedicated to the principles of inclusion and informed consent. They are working to alleviate poverty among their ranks and to educate the public about mental illness.

People First. A national organization of intellectually disabled people promoting equality and opportunity for all persons who have been labeled mentally handicapped. They run the organization themselves. Sometimes they select and consult advisors to help them interpret or simplify issues and communications so the group can function and make its own decisions.

An International Voice

Throughout the 1970s disabled Canadians tried to get international clout by lobbying Rehabilitation International to include equal numbers of disabled delegates in decision making.

Rehabilitation International (RI) was to the world what CRCD was to Canada. This global partnership of rehabilitation organizations was founded in 1922 as the International Society for Crippled Children but changed its name when it changed its mandate to include adults. It tended to view disabled people as "sick and childlike patients who needed professionals to care for them from cradle to grave."[17] CRCD was a member.

By 1980 at the RI World Congress in Winnipeg, COPOH (CCD) had become a member as well and increasing numbers of disabled delegates were attending these events. COPOH helped organize the congress and sent fifty disabled delegates. RI's practices and attitudes affected disabled people and they wanted to have a say in their own destinies. Often they knew better than their doctors, physiotherapists and social workers how to manage their disabilities so to them it was logical to have equal status with their service providers in setting policy.

However, the rehabilitation professionals didn't recognize them as experts or equals. They rejected an amendment from the Swedish delegation proposing for RI the equal representation Sweden already practised both at home and in its delegate selection. Instead RI approved only token representation by disabled people.

In response the 300 disabled delegates met outside the congress and decided to form their own world-wide body, defying the patronizing doubts of the majority of RI's professional delegates. The following year they succeeded with the first World Congress of Disabled Peoples' International in Singapore, a declaration of independence appropriately capping the United Nations International Year of the Disabled.[18]

Membership and Influence

The influence and effectiveness of the Canadian provincial members of CCD exceed their immediate memberships. Enrollment figures reflect, not only the degree of interest, but also the rules governing membership. Some provincial organizations exclude able-bodied people from voting while others allow full membership privileges to those sponsored by a disabled person. Some even include like-minded able-bodied people as a minority on their boards.[19] The groups extend their effectiveness by forming temporary or permanent alliances with other groups having the same goals.

The provincial groups also say their influence includes disabled people who choose not to take out a membership. Many of these people believe in and pursue the goals of consumerism and independent living in their individual lives but do not want to be a part of public advocacy.[20]

CCD and most of the provincial groups stick to advocacy and leave services to the agencies or their own independent living centres. Prince Edward Island, however, both advocates and provides services, responding to the lack of agencies in their tiny province. British Columbia will assist individuals having trouble getting or keeping a job but otherwise also confines itself to its lobby function. Each provincial group is totally autonomous.

Language: Naming Themselves

The names and language used by disabled people and their organizations have evolved with their self awareness.

When they first chose names they outright rejected the word "cripple" as it appeared in the name of the Winnipeg agency, the Society for Crippled Children and Adults. This word has become synonymous with the oppressive atmosphere and attitudes they are trying to shake off.

At first they substituted "the handicapped" before they developed the present definition of handicap as defined below. In most instances the preposition "for" implied dependency on able-bodied people so they used "of" instead, as in the Manitoba League of the Physically Handicapped.

Just as members of visible minorities have changed their group nomenclature as they clarified their thinking about themselves, so disabled people altered their terminology several times. "The handicapped," which omitted their humanity making their disabilities into a noun defining their whole identities, became "persons with disabilities" in an effort to put their human status ahead of their disabilities.

Research supports attaching the word "person" to the disability adjective. People reacted more negatively to "blindness" or "physical handicap" than to "blind people" or "physically handicapped people" in a classic study cited by author and psychologist, Beatrice A. Wright. "That the condition itself was evaluated far more negatively than were people with the condition is not surprising." She attributed the difference to the moderating context the person provided for the disability.[21]

In the new self-descriptive vocabulary, impairments, handicaps and disabilities were redefined. The World Health Organization's definitions say, "Impairments are disturbances at the level of the organ," a disability "describes a functional limitation or activity restriction caused by an impairment" and a handicap is "any disadvantage for a given individual, resulting from an impairment or a disability, that limits or prevents the fulfillment of a role that is normal for that individual."[22] Disabled people are trying to change these definitions. They say handicaps are the physical barriers while disabilities are a person's physical or mental limitations; for example, to a wheelchair user, stairs would be a handicap.

"Wheelchair bound" or "confined to a wheelchair" was replaced with "wheelchair user" to eliminate the emphasis on limitations and focus instead on consumerism and the liberating effect a wheelchair has on someone who would be truly restricted without one. And to some, able-bodied people became TABs or temporarily able-bodied.

They prefer "survivor" to "victim" because the latter plays to the stereotype of disability being a perpetual tragedy. The former has positive connotations of living through a struggle, perhaps being permanently marked by it, but nevertheless going on to lead a satisfying life. While Tracy Latimer is described as a victim in this book, it is as a victim of murder, not her disabilities.

Most importantly, using any disability descriptor is inappropriate and misleading if the topic does not involve disability. As was shown in the first two chapters, this was done repeatedly in the Latimer case, in the courts and particularly in the media even while those using these descriptors protested that this case was not about disability.

After they had developed a vocabulary to fit their revised thinking, they changed the names of their organizations. The Alberta group has had four names. The initial Alberta Committee of Action Groups for the Disabled became the Alberta Committee of Consumer Groups of Disabled Persons in 1982, the Alberta Committee of Disabled Citizens in 1986, and finally the Alberta Committee of Citizens with Disabilities in 1990.

And along the way their thinking found its way beyond their immediate circles into the same agencies and other organizations that had formerly defined them. The Society for Crippled Children and Adults, which employed several disabled professionals active in the Manitoba League of the Physically Handicapped, eventually became the Society for Manitobans with Disabilities and its literature now uses the new terminology.

Disabled activists changed their thinking about alliances between different types of disability. In Manitoba the original organization was restricted to issues surrounding people with physical disabilities but they gradually realized that many of the barriers they faced were similar to those confronting people with mental or intellectual disabilities. Those barriers were rooted in the attitudes of the dominant population. The new official names reflected this inclusiveness as well.

But the attitudes of the world outside these organizations didn't keep pace with the vocabulary and name changes. To most, these were merely euphemisms masking hard reality. To some it was political correctness, just so many new words to show their superior level of awareness, their ability to keep up with the fashion in words and sentiment. The words were just a trend, a style to be discarded when the next one came along, like clothing or hairstyles.

But to disabled people these changes were a reflection of who they were, who they had become. Acquiring their own words to fit their own concepts was as important as naming a child. They were naming a new reality.

Their vocabulary is likely not cast in stone. As long as disabled people continue to wrestle with a language created by able-bodied people, the evolution of self expression will continue. Even now some like Bev Mathiessen of Alberta are unhappy with the term "consumer." She prefers "citizen" which implies rights and responsibilities and the Alberta group's current name includes that word.

Finances

Money is always a problem with any self-help organization but particularly for those run by disabled people. Always wary of distorting their message with their methods, these groups were careful in their fundraising. Not only did they have to find money, they had to do it in a manner compatible with their philosophy, not an easy task when the usual private sources were charity-oriented and public sources were funnelled through the health care system. They couldn't turn to their own constituency for much because disabled people were generally poor.

From their inception the organizations have relied largely on government grants. Laurie Beachell estimates that 90 percent of CCD's income is from the federal government. A major disadvantage of this reliance is being at the mercy of political moods and economic downturns. In 1996, during the height of the fiscal restraint period, CCD was told by the federal government that by the year 2000 they would lose all their government financial support. Had that happened this voice on national issues would have been silenced and the government would have reneged on its responsibility to ensure equal opportunity for disadvantaged groups.

Without the government they would have been forced to turn either to private fund-raising companies, which take at least half of all money collected, or to their own efforts which would have sapped most of their human and financial resources. Beachell said competition for money is onerous. They fought the government decision, won, and with the federal budget being balanced, there are even hints of an eventual reversal in their fortunes, although government obfuscation like changing program names and sources makes progress difficult to track.

These groups prefer to apply for money from government departments designated for all citizens, not just for disabled Canadians or under health categories; it does not make sense to fund employment programs for disabled people under health but governments have stubbornly persisted in dumping it and every other disability-related issue there.

As mentioned earlier in this chapter, the self-advocacy organizations are devising fund-raising events conveying the image they want to project, such as the Manitoba Independent Living Resource Centre's kite festival with its slogan, "Come fly with us."

Achievements

Many early leaders of the movement were young, mobility-impaired students and professionals who had managed to become educated or even employed in spite of the odds stacked against them, or who had become disabled after becoming educated and employed. The first issues they tackled were education, employment, public relations, human rights and accessibility in transportation, housing and public buildings.

Throughout the 1980s the Canadian organizations expanded their influence provincially and nationally. Travel became easier. Cities inserted curb cuts at street corners and their transit systems added vans equipped to accommodate wheelchair passengers heading to work, doctors' appointments, grocery shopping or entertainment. Airlines became more accessible to wheelchair users and the terminals installed visual displays for travellers who couldn't hear announcements over a public address system. No longer did disabled railroad passengers have to ride in the baggage cars at full fare when regular coaches could not accommodate their needs. Parking lots sprouted handicapped parking spaces near major entrances to public buildings, a vital feature in Canada's winter months.

Provincial and federal building codes were revised to include such accommodations as ramped entrances, wider doors and wheelchair accessible stalls in washrooms. These codes, however, are only as good as their enforcement and disabled people had to fight for that as well. When the Manitoba Building Code was revised to dictate accessibility in new buildings, the code exempted those who could demonstrate that compliance would be prohibitively expensive.

With increased accessibility came increased visibility which some advocates view as a public relations tool in its own right. The more people saw disabled people at school, at work, out shopping or in the theatres and restaurants, the less they felt the urge to "rubber-neck" at someone in a wheelchair.

Activists established independent living centres where disabled people could get consumer-style help in accessing services without having to resume the role of children or subject themselves to an agency evaluation. The centre in Winnipeg helped pilot a new approach to home-care where the recipients are assessed for the amount of help they need and are then given the money to hire their own staff for those hours. The new method minimizes service overlap and allows disabled people to find staff compatible with their needs. The portable services can be transferred from home to work or elsewhere, as negotiated between the employer and employee, and this opens up job opportunities for greater numbers of severely disabled people.

A Voice Unheard

As far as the activist groups are concerned, the agencies whose patronizing approach fueled their movement have retreated into the background. The dominance they exerted over their clients has been replaced with a more collaborative approach. Many now have disabled people on their boards and are hiring them for administrative positions.

Increased awareness of the potential of disabled people has led to technological advances specifically for these needs. However, although technology promises much, it also hinders. DOS computer operating systems placed blind computer programmers and analysts on an equal footing with their sighted colleagues but the advent of visually oriented systems such as Windows has put some blind people out of work and made computer operations more difficult for all of them. Mel Graham says blind people are constantly scrambling to adapt the new programs to their auditory methods.

Working in advocacy organizations has educated disabled people in leadership. In 1980 Allan Simpson wrote, "few disabled people in Canada have been aware of how the political/bureaucratic process can be made to work for a community need."[23] Few had served on boards or councils or held public office but through these groups many more have become aware of our democratic system and how to make it work for them.

In the 1991 Health and Activity Limitation Survey (HALS), Statistics Canada suggested a growing acceptance of disability as one explanation for the increased number of Canadians willing to describe themselves as disabled. The first survey in 1986 found 10.4 percent of Canadians between the ages of fifteen and sixty-four had disabilities while in 1991 the percentage had increased to 12.7. Of the total population of Canada more than 16 percent identified themselves as disabled.[24] Of those, just over half were classified as mildly disabled, a third were moderately and about 15 percent severely disabled.

Disabled children are attending local schools and interacting with their able-bodied peers. The education statistics in the two HALS surveys, while not enough to be a trend, tantalizingly suggest an improvement in education levels among disabled people (see Table 1). Only the two surveys have been done so far; apparently other studies have been victims of cutbacks, so long-term trends in these areas cannot be tracked.

With higher education comes more employment opportunities. HALS found an increased employment rate among disabled people to 48 percent in 1991 from 40 percent in 1986. This is compared with an increase of only 3 percent in the general population. The biggest increase—10 percent—was among disabled females while the employment rate among disabled males rose 8 percent.

In 1991 the federal Liberal government announced the National

Table 1

All persons with disabilities (mild, moderate, severe)		
	1991	1986
no formal schooling	2%	3%
primary level only	18%	26%
secondary level	45%	40%
some post-secondary	11%	16%
certificate or diploma	19%	10%
university degree	6%	5%
Among the population without disabilities		
	1991	1986 (NA)
no formal schooling	less than 1%	
primary level only	8%	
secondary level	43%	
some post-secondary	13%	
certificate or diploma	22%	
university degree	14%	

Source: Statistics Canada, *Health and Activity Limitation Survey (HALS)*, pp. xvii–xviii.

Strategy for the Integration of Persons with Disabilities (NSIPD), an attempt to integrate disabled Canadians into the government mainstream. Instead of the traditional approach of shoving all disability concerns into the health department, this initiative distributed these issues to eleven federal departments and agencies.[25] While its 1995 report indicated progress in all departments, NSIPD did not find much economic integration. Still it recommended continuing the strategy. Disabled people were consulted in planning it so to some extent their voice is being heard in government.

But the most important achievement was inclusion of disabled people's rights in all the provincial bills of rights and most significantly in the federal Charter of Rights and Freedoms in 1985. Without that inclusion all the advances they had made since the mid-1970s could be reversed or ignored without any recourse. That is exactly what Justice Noble tried to do in Robert Latimer's second trial and that was another reason why disabled activists couldn't ignore his decision. Without the recognition of their rights as citizens, they would once again be as vulnerable

Table 2

Rate of employment		
	1991	1986
persons with disabilities	48%	40%
persons without disabilities	73%	70%
Rate of unemployment		
	1991	1986
persons with disabilities	8%	7%
persons without disabilities	8%	8%
Percentage of workers not in the labour force, neither employed nor unemployed		
	1991	1986
persons with disabilities	44%	51%
persons without disabilities	19%	NA

Source: *Health and Activity Limitation Survey (HALS)* Statistics Canada, pp. xi – xii.

as they had been in the dark ages of the nineteenth and early twentieth century.

The advocacy groups involved in the Latimer case didn't have the resources to fight for every disabled murder victim but this case was crucial. They had to fight it even though it forced them to go over ground they had already covered, to again fight battles they thought they had won: their worth as human beings, their place in the Charter and their place in Canadian society.

The Job Ahead

For these self-advocacy groups the Latimer case has not been the only fight. Laurie Beachell describes the 1990s as a decade of scrambling to keep what the disabled community won in previous decades.

The emphasis on government fiscal responsibility has taken its toll. Although cutbacks may not have deliberately targeted vulnerable populations, these groups feel privation more quickly and profoundly than affluent segments of society. "Same treatment does not translate into equal treatment," Beachell said. Also, government practices of shifting funding definitions and sources makes it difficult to trace how much has been taken away or when these organizations will have recovered lost ground. "You can't track the cuts directly."

Coming Out of the Attic

The reinstatement of the Health and Ability Limitation Survey in the next census is important. Without it, data collection and research by and about disabled people is severely hampered. As with the women's movement, disabled researchers and advocates also deserve the right to study the progress of their own groups and use the findings to push for improvements in their own lives. This too is part of finding their voice and being heard.

Another perpetual concern is acquiring and maintaining support services and delivery systems with more input from those using the services, as in public education. In February 1997 the Supreme Court ruled against twelve-year-old Emily Eaton's parents and disabled intervenors who were trying to prevent her removal from the neighbourhood school in Brant County, Ontario to a special classroom. The reasons given for the ruling did not examine possible explanations for the behaviour that had prompted the struggle between the parents and the education system. Emily's crying, sleeping in class and vocalizing were presumed to be the result of a mismatch between her level of ability and her school environment. However, the ruling did not mention an investigation into whether the general atmosphere in the school had been a truly accepting one or try to find out why Emily had been crying. Surely that would have been done for other children.[26]

Crimes against disabled people need to be brought out of the closet. The Latimer case has shown that the Canadian justice system must become more aware of and responsive to crimes against disabled individuals. Insp. Ken Biener of the Winnipeg police was quoted by the Winnipeg *Free Press* in December 1998 saying, "abuse of the disabled is 'stunningly under-reported' and there need to be officers trained in detecting problems before they escalate."[27] The same article said Biener expects to have a vulnerable persons unit in place by fall 1999. It was one of Court of Queen's Bench Justice Perry Schulman's recommendations after an inquiry into the deaths of Roy and Rhonda Lavoie following years of domestic violence. The unit would be called into cases involving vulnerable persons, such as children, seniors and disabled individuals. However, better tracking of such incidents is also necessary. It must start with the recognition that the Latimer case was indeed murder punishable under the same laws as other murders. Without such recognition cases like the Latimer murder might not even be classified as a violent crime and statistics would not be accurate.

Human rights are an issue at home and abroad. Internationally, the Canadian government says it intends to promote human rights. Such legislation may be on the books in Canada and may be a priority for the Canadian Foreign Affairs Minister Lloyd Axworthy, but disability issues are not as high on his agenda as children, freedom of religion and freedom of the media. Although he gave passing mention to disabled people in his December 17, 1998 article to the Winnipeg *Free Press* marking the fiftieth anniversary of the United Nations Universal Declaration of Human Rights, he did not include them in the three priorities he is promoting internationally.[28] The Latimer case shows that the government cannot afford to relax on disability issues at home or abroad. Disabled people are vulnerable everywhere.

Before Canadians can truly support the disabled segment of society they need to be reading from the same page as those receiving their support. Simple awareness is not enough; attitudes also have to change. Disabled people can make dramatic progress but, as long as their fellow citizens don't follow or understand their pilgrimage, the powerless remain as defenceless as Tracy Latimer.

Most of all, the voices of disabled citizens aware of the options in independent living should be heard in every aspect of society that can affect their lives, especially areas like medicine, law and ethics which become involved in life-and-death decisions. The experts being consulted now are not always able to speak knowledgeably to these issues. Informed disabled people can.

Notes

1. For a more extensive discussion of this and other issues in this brief history of disability, see Richard Atlick, *Victorian People and Ideas;* Derek Fraser, *The New Poor Law in the Nineteenth Century*; Boyd Hilton, *The Age of Atonement*; Angus MaLaren, *Our Own Master Race* and Robert Scott, *The Making of Blind Men.*
2. Frederick H. Lowy et al., (1993) *Canadian Physicians and Euthanasia*, Ottawa: Canadian Medical Association.
3. Heather Pringle, "Alberta Barren," p. 74.
4. Dick Sobsey, "The Media and Robert Latimer," p. 40.
5. BBC2 (May 2, 1991). One in Four.
6. Dick Sobsey, "The Media and Robert Latimer," p. 40–41.
7. Diane Driedger, "Organizing for Change," p. 2.
8. Jim Derksen, "The Disabled Consumer Movement," p. 5.
9. Jim Derksen, "The Disabled Consumer Movement," p. 4.
10. Anne Mullens, *Timely Death,* p. 86.
11. Medical and technological advances are often credited for the increased numbers of disabled people. That kind of thinking tends to paint the Tracy Latimers as a drain on society, using valuable resources that could better be used by more productive citizens. However, medicine and rehabilitation are also indebted to the people they serve. The economic law of supply and demand might credit the increased demand—the greater number of disabled people—for the increased supply of medical and technological advances. Many industries and jobs connected to this area may well be the result of the increased rate of disability. The tenacious survival of the

Tracy Latimers may force medicine and rehabilitation to new frontiers and more innovation so perhaps it would be wiser to simply acknowledge a symbiotic relationship between disability and medical technology and abandon the implicit scapegoating of people like Tracy.

12. Diane Driedger, "Organizing for Change," pp. 2–3.
13. Diane Driedger, "Organizing for Change," p. 6.
14. Diane Driedger, "Organizing for Change," p. 6.
15. Allan J. Simpson, "Consumer Groups," pp. 9 and 10.
16. Diane Driedger, "Organizing for Change," pp. 3–5.
17. Diane Driedger, *The Last Civil Rights Movement,* p. 28.
18. Diane Driedger, *The Last Civil Rights Movement*, p. 30–37.
19. Allan J. Simpson, "Consumer Groups," p. 7.
20. Allan J. Simpson, "Consumer Groups," p. 7.
21. Federal/Provincial/Territorial Ministers Responsible for Social Services, "In Unison," Appendix A, p. 28.
22. Beatrice A. Wright, "Attitudes and the Fundamental Negative Bias," p. 6.
23. Allan J. Simpson, "Consumer Groups," p. 23.
24. Statistics Canada, HALS *Survey,* p. xi.
25. Goss Gilroy Inc., Management Consultants, "Interdepartmental Evaluation of the National Strategy for the Integration of Persons with Disabilities." The departments and agencies were: Canadian Heritage, Canada Mortgage and Housing Corporation, Health Canada, Human Resources Development Canada, Indian and Northern Affairs, Industry Canada, Justice Canada, National Library, National Transportation Agency, Transport Canada and the Treasury Board Secretariat.
26. Eaton v. Brant County Board of Education, Supreme Court of Canada.
27. Mike McIntyre (December 15, 1998). "Slaying shows need for police unit to aid the vulnerable: officer." Winnipeg *Free Press,* A4.
28. Lloyd Axworthy (December 17, 1998). "Canada at forefront in human rights." Winnipeg *Free Press*, A15.

Chapter Four

Living with Disability

In 1992 Mike Rosner was admitted to a Winnipeg hospital with severe pneumonia. Shortly after arriving at intensive care the doctors told him he had only hours, at most a few days to live. "They inquired about whether I wanted them to treat me aggressively," he said.

Mike, a lifelong wheelchair user, has spiral muscular atrophy type two, a neuro-muscular disorder present from birth but manifesting itself at about age one. It is one of about forty neuro-muscular disorders classified as muscular dystrophy or MD; all are very different from each other.

Mike was surprised. He had assumed that aggressive treatment was the reason one goes to hospital. About four or five doctors each tried to convince him "that I ought to let nature take its course." They told him if he did survive, his quality of life would be so poor as to not be worthwhile. "They painted a very bleak picture."

They said treatment would involve a tracheotomy—the insertion of a breathing tube into the trachea through the neck—and other surgery, that he would have to have a feeding tube, that resuscitation would be too hard on him, that his strength wouldn't return.

They assumed he wasn't an active person. He had helped found the Manitoba League of Persons with Disabilities and before this bout of pneumonia he had been in the final planning stages of moving to independent living. A suite in a housing co-op had opened up just before he got sick. When he told the doctors he had indeed been active, they said he could forget all that now, including independent living. If he opted for aggressive treatment he would spend the rest of his life in a hospital.

"They painted an equally rosy picture of helping me die." They would make sure he had no pain and make him comfortable. "It sounded like they would really attend to me. They made it sound pretty nice."

He became angry despite his weakened state. "I was insulted that they would think this in the first place," he said. "It was because I was disabled." He decided to go for the treatment to spite them. He did have the tracheotomy and still uses a ventilator but didn't need a feeding tube and six years later at age forty-one still didn't need it.

He spent three weeks in intensive care and three months at Riverview Health Centre, a long-term care facility in Winnipeg. After he recovered he had an uphill battle to get out of hospital to the independent life he had planned. Home care had written him off, cancelling his orderlies. It took a lot of lobbying with help and letters from the Independent Living Resource Centre and others to make his point but in April 1993 he disproved his doctor's pessimistic predictions and began life away from his parental home and institutions. Although his condition has not allowed him to hold a job either before or after this incident, he has put his university education to good use in consulting, volunteer work and in managing his own life.

Attitudes Toward Persons with Disabilities

Although types of disability are innumerable and the coping skills for dealing with them are unique to each condition and to each person, they all have one common element: the prevalent attitudes of able-bodied people toward them. People with impairments, particularly noticeable ones, often say their limitations are easier to live with than other people's prejudice, even when the disablement includes pain and disfiguring surgeries.

Nancy Weinberg, a contributor to Harold Yuker's book on attitudes toward disabled people, found that able-bodied people stick to their misguided assumptions about physical and mental impairments even in the face of contradicting evidence. When she informally related research revealing that not all disabled individuals would opt to become able-bodied if given the opportunity, her listeners refused to believe her. They insisted the research must be wrong.[1]

The researchers repeated the experiments with modifications to address the criticism but the results were the same. Analysis showed that these unexpected attitudes were the product of the subjects' perceptions of themselves and whether the disabilities interfered with or actually helped them attain their goals. A deaf stunt woman saw her hearing deficiency as an asset because it helped her concentrate on her job; to her the disability was a challenge to be conquered like the stunts she performed in her work. Others liked who they were and what they had learned as a result of their disabilities; they feared becoming able-bodied would change their outlook.

Disabled individuals' attitudes toward their own lives are similar to those of able-bodied persons to theirs. Weinberg wrote, "While society tends to view disability as a continuing tragedy, we found that attitudes of disabled persons seem to be the same as those of any group of individuals who try to adapt to a difficult situation.... A few people view it negatively, a few find something positive in it, and the majority fall in between."[2]

Beatrice A. Wright cited research on the "fortune phenomenon" which asked subjects to rate themselves and others on how fortunate they are. It revealed "the ease with which devalued groups are regarded as unfortunate, despite the fact that the members of those groups do not view themselves as unfortunate."[3]

Mike Rosner's experience shows that even medical professionals are not necessarily free of bias toward disabled people. Beatrice Wright attributes this attitude to a clinical emphasis on problems. She wrote, "Being problem-oriented, the clinician easily concentrates on pathology, dysfunction, and troubles, to the neglect of discovering those important assets in the person and resources in the environment that must be drawn upon in the best problem-solving efforts."[4]

Nor is research about disability immune to this bias. According to Michael Oliver and Priscilla Anderson writing in the *British Medical Journal*, health research "focuses on searches for cures, means of reducing impairments, or assessments of clinical interventions."[5] It is suspicious of involving subjects for fear of bias and yet uses subjective terms like suffering and victim "as if they are accurate descriptions and not untested, biased assumptions which many disabled people do not experience." These authors said most funding goes to such "positivist" research.

Another of the five types of disability research identified by these authors, functionalism, "confuses impairment and disability with the sick role." By emphasizing compliance and a desire to get well it implies that there is perpetually something wrong with the disabled person, thereby linking disability with social deviance and supporting the continued dominance of professionals. Other types of research, social constructionism and postmodernism, also either fall short of including the whole person within society or are too simplistic in their approaches.

The views of disabled people often conflict with research done about them from a clinical perspective. Oliver and Anderson say the views of disabled people have come to be called social oppression theory and have been recorded only within the last twenty years. Critical theory research links disability problems with social oppression and solutions with social action. Rather than concentrating on making the individual fit society through surgery, technology or rehabilitation, this approach would alter society to include the individual: for example, rather than solve the problem of transportation for wheelchair users by creating a parallel transportation system, it would make the existing public transportation system wheelchair accessible.

The descriptions of Tracy Latimer in court revealed positivist and functionalist attitudes, repeatedly using words such as "suffering," stressing her body's deviation from the norm and relying on professional assessments of her prospects rather than the experiences of disabled people.

Living with Disability

For Mike Rosner, the positivist and functionalist attitudes nearly ended his life prematurely. His experience also graphically demonstrates that the major participants in the Latimer case, such as Tracy's parents, the defence counsel, witnesses, judges, juries and the media, are not unusual in their views that disability, dependency and pain bring a tortured existence devoid of meaning and value. Public opinion has clearly been on the side of Robert Latimer.

Nor are these attitudes directed only toward those with severe disabilities. This phenomenon can target people with lesser impairments or members of other minorities. And everyone is susceptible to the lure of devaluing another human being, to the sense of superiority it brings. Just as anyone can be a victim of a negative bias, so can anyone be the offender.

This devaluation is most likely to occur under the conditions observed by Wright and noted in earlier chapters: if a feature stands out, is perceived as negative and appears in a sparse context, internal or external, then the result will be a fundamental negative bias which "steers perception, thought, and feeling along negative lines to such a degree that positives remain hidden."[6]

If strangers notice nothing but a person's faults, they will see nothing else, assume there is nothing else to know and form negative opinions based on that limited, one-sided knowledge. Malicious gossip, for example, usually isolates the rejected aspects of the targeted person from other characteristics. When the discrimination involves a group, results can include racism, sexism, homophobia or the phenomenon some disabled people call able-ism.

A living will form purchased in a stationery shop shows this pervasive negative bias against disability. It says death is preferable to any disability: "If the situation should arise in which there is no reasonable expectation of my recovery from physical or mental disability, then I request that ... I be allowed to die." It says the signatory does not fear death as much as "deterioration, dependence and hopeless pain."[7] It lumps all disabilities together, regardless of type or severity, disregarding the fact that permanent disabilities are incurable and people do not recover from them but rather learn to live with them. If this document were legally binding, medical care-givers could interpret it at their own discretion with impunity unless the signatory had the foresight and medical knowledge to limit the will to specific situations.

This form has the same underlying attitude as the court proceedings in and the media approach to the Latimer case. Most trial participants and observers presumed that disabilities, and to a lesser degree pain, are more difficult to face than death. They concluded Tracy's murder was compassionate, that it relieved her from a life of pain when evidence clearly showed that her pain was periodic and treatable, and that she was happy most of the time.

It was a conclusion formulated on the basis Wright described. It was founded on only those features most obvious and distasteful to the observers. To Latimer sympathizers, the only relevant aspects of Tracy were her disabilities and pain so they dwelt on these features to the complete exclusion of her personality and pleasures. To them Tracy was a stranger and they made no effort to get to know her. Her life outside hospitals and doctors' offices didn't exist for them, even when it was placed before them by the second prosecution. Her own mother, who provided most of her care but who seemed to remain a stranger to disability issues, downplayed any evidence of Tracy's intelligence and focussed instead on the bleakness of her life. By looking only at her difficulties and none of her joy the observers then saw nothing but a dreary existence. They were negatively biased against Tracy.

Only the disabled advocates and their supporters realized what was happening but they, too, were seen in the light of the central disability prejudice. Because the court was blind to the relevance of disability, the advocates and their arguments were also dismissed as irrelevant, often quite openly, such as in the *Star Phoenix* editorial mentioned above.

The Stewarts

The Latimer case touched the lives of many disabled Canadians, particularly those living with conditions similar to Tracy's. Brian and Anne Stewart of the St. Andrews municipality north of Winnipeg are one of those families. Brian has cerebral palsy. They have discussed Tracy's situation and death with their children but their attitude toward disability is as positive as the Latimers' is negative. They tackle disability as just another problem of everyday life.

The Stewarts have seven youngsters, four of them foster children. Of the four "chosen" ones, as they call them, three have cerebral palsy; two have severe spastic quadriplegia like Tracy and also cannot walk, talk or feed themselves. The three children born to them—Lucas, Nicholas and Eva Marie—are able-bodied. Since cerebral palsy is not a genetic disorder, children born to people with this disorder do not have a significantly greater risk of having it than children in the general population.

The family's major obstacle quickly becomes evident as they speak of their lives together. Their greatest hurdle has been the attitudes of the ignorant and prejudiced. While their descriptions of disabilities are matter-of-fact, when the topic switches to attitudes the whole family becomes animated, upset but eager to tell this other story, the one omitted from most accounts about people like them.

They know what most disabled people learn: just as beauty is in the eye of the beholder, so is much of the horror of disability. Nobody asks to become disabled but most disabled persons are not preoccupied with escaping their conditions. They simply learn to live with their situations as their able-bodied friends and neighbours learn to live with theirs.

Jon Stewart, who was twelve in 1998, faces most of the physical conditions the Latimers and the media found so horrifying in Tracy. Like her, he has difficulty eating enough to sustain his growing body; a simple lunch of a sandwich and a drink will take an hour or longer to eat. He has also had many of the surgeries Tracy had and he faces more.

Jon's permanent foster parents value his life. In part their acceptance comes from personal experience. Anne was adopted and said a few relatives made her feel she didn't belong. Brian himself has cerebral palsy severe enough that when he was a child no one expected him to achieve much. "It was never anticipated when Brian was in elementary school that he would work, let alone go to university," said Anne.

Brian told a vigil for Tracy held in Winnipeg in 1995 that, "Forty plus years ago my parents were told not to take me home. Those concerned for my parents' well-being, the medical profession, could not see my life as being worth living.... their vision was that I would not have a future and they did not, would not, or could not, see a place in the community for me."[8]

Certainly no one would have expected him to create his own firm and become its executive director, to own and drive a vehicle or to marry and have a family. He did all of that. Yet when Brian wanted to get a driver's license, the doctor he had seen all his life refused to sign the necessary papers, saying Brian didn't need to drive. He changed doctors and got the licence in 1980.

The mental capabilities of non-verbal people are hard to assess but Brian and Anne made the effort to look for evidence of their children's abilities and found that they could not be determined simply by the general level of impairment. As the British Columbia Cerebral Palsy Association said in its web site, just because someone with CP is unable to speak does not mean that he or she has nothing to say; the degree of physical disability does not indicate the level of intelligence.

The Stewarts had to fight to have Jon enrolled in the local school but once there he revealed his learning capacity. In 1998 he was in grade seven, keeping up with his classmates in the regular language arts program. He shows his comprehension by answering yes/no or multiple choice questions on his computer. While he can use sentences, they take too long and are too exhausting for him to write for prolonged periods. In June 1999 the computer voice attached to his wheelchair demonstrated Jon's ability to "speak" by relating part of Brian's essay at the launch of CCD's book in Winnipeg.

Noah joined the family at the age of ten in 1992. He occasionally visits his birth mother and younger brother, his "other family" as the Stewarts call them. He also cannot walk, talk or feed himself. However, where Jon catches on to jokes and anticipates action on television, Noah tends to see the world in black and white. Unexpected changes leave him frustrated and emotionally out of control. "He's quite a character," Anne said, smiling calmly.

For now, one of Noah's independent living goals is to communicate his needs to his attendants. Giving accurate instructions requires breaking down a task into smaller sequential components. The Stewarts found that home economics provided many opportunities for learning these skills so in the middle grades Noah took home economics. When he reached the higher grades the school wouldn't allow him to enroll in that course on that basis. Again the Stewarts fought and won.

Then there is Ericka. She too has cerebral palsy and cannot speak although she can walk and vocalizes a lot. Brian said when she was born the doctors put a do-not resuscitate order on her chart but the nurses ignored it. "And we're glad they did," said Anne. "So is Ericka."

Ericka spent the first six months of her life in hospital. She was born in 1983 with two of the many risk factors for cerebral palsy: it was a multiple birth and she weighed only one and a half pounds at birth. She is blind and learning disabled. She had one epileptic seizure at age ten but none since.

Ericka and Jon both arrived at the Stewarts as infants so this is the only home they have ever known. When Jon was about to enter grade three they moved to the country from Winnipeg with Brian commuting to his work in the city. They moved because of the attitudes they faced in Winnipeg. Although the Stewarts were trying to teach her socially acceptable behaviour, Ericka's vocalizing and "gyrations," as Anne calls her movements, attracted attention. Even their own back yard did not provide enough privacy to let her relax and be herself. Their six-foot fence wasn't high enough to keep out prying eyes and the taunts of ignorant children. Walks around the block were no pleasure. They felt like they were under house arrest. Like celebrities they had no protection from curiosity seekers, except instead of being cheered they were jeered.

In that school division the separate-but-equal credo reigned as it did against black people in 1960s Mississippi, only here it segregated disabled children from able-bodied ones, so in the spring of 1991 the

Living with Disability

Stewarts moved to their present large house overlooking the Red River. The lot was bigger than a city lot with tall trees and fairly dense bush providing shelter.

Yet even here, away from claustrophobic urban yards, the widespread, persistent misconceptions about cerebral palsy surfaced. About a year after they moved in, a general practitioner who lived down the road tried to comfort Anne. When Anne, bewildered, asked why, she found out the doctor said she felt sorry for her because Brian was dying of multiple sclerosis. Anne replied that he has cerebral palsy, not MS, and that he was not dying, but the doctor breezily dismissed her clarification saying the two are very similar.

Anne is still amazed that a doctor could be so ignorant about two different and fairly common conditions. MS is a chronic degenerative disease of the central nervous system, in some people progressing slowly and intermittently, in others swiftly and steadily. In MS, patches of the myelin sheath around nerve fibres are gradually lost. Symptoms usually first appear when the person is between twenty and forty years of age.

Cerebral palsy is not degenerative nor terminal although it can bring complications which in very severe cases can be life-threatening. Although it is also a neurological disorder, the causes are completely different from MS. Cerebral palsy is caused by damage to the developing brain either before birth or up to the age of three or four. Brain damage occurring later in life from strokes, accidents or illness, is not called cerebral palsy although it can produce similar symptoms. Dr. Richard Snyder told the *Globe and Mail* that cerebral palsy occurs in about one or two children in a thousand.

Despite the ignorance of their physician neighbour, the Stewarts found the St. Andrews neighbourhood somewhat better than Winnipeg and they managed to get on friendly terms with some local residents. They thought things were looking up. After living there for seven years without Brian showing any signs of deterioration, neighbours no longer assumed he was dying and the children were even able to make some friends.

However, the doctor incident was not the only unwelcome event in their new home. Anne said on April 1, 1998 a representative of the district planning board knocked on the door and "aggressively" informed them that group homes are not allowed in the area. Anne's protests that theirs is not a group home but a foster family fell on deaf ears. The municipal bylaw did not distinguish between the two.

After eight days of phone calls and hassles that spoiled Easter for the whole family and left Anne feeling sick to her stomach, the municipality backed off, saying it would rewrite the bylaw by September, 1998.

However, that victory came only after Child and Family Services threatened legal action. To the Stewarts it was a hollow victory. The municipality had acted without investigation and on a single complaint from a newcomer to the community.

By December, 1998, the bylaw had not been rewritten, the municipal council members had changed and the planning board that had confronted the Stewarts in order to enforce the bylaw was saying there was no guarantee the new council would adopt the board's recommendations. It expected the Stewarts to lobby again for the changes to local regulations.

Was it the disabilities? Was it that their four foster children are of native ancestry? Or was it a combination of the two? In the end did it matter? Prejudice is prejudice. Here, too, they were unwanted, targeted and almost alone against the world.

It is probably no accident that their foster children are all native. According to a report on international compliance with the United Nations Standard Rules for the Equalization of Opportunities for Persons with Disabilities, because the federal Department of Indian Affairs has no formal policy for the education of disabled children living on reserves, the onus is on band councils to provide it. However, the report said, "Band councils are not bound by any federal or provincial policies on inclusive or integrated education for students with disabilities." Consequently, special education services are not available on reserves and "Aboriginal parents of children with disabilities living on reserve must relinquish guardianship of their children in order for them to be eligible for provincially funded special education services." Off reserve these services are the same for native children as for others. The report by Deborah Stienstra, who teaches politics at the University of Winnipeg, and Patrick Kellerman, a past project officer for Disabled Peoples International said Canada signed the UN agreement in 1993.[9]

The Stewarts' able-bodied children also feel the sting of the bias against their family. Eva Marie, born in 1985, said the family name alone is enough to stigmatize them and she resents the fact that, whenever a new disabled child appears at school, it is assumed the Stewarts have another addition.

But instead of resenting her foster siblings she has adopted her parents' open, accepting attitude toward those who are different. She has become a staunch advocate for them, even helping Jon retaliate against the children who kick his wheelchair tires. She jokingly says she distracts them while Jon runs over them.

Nick, three years older than Eva Marie, also keenly feels the slight. He admitted it is easy to dissociate himself from the family in public. In a mall he can walk with his father and no one will guess the relationship between them. He is reluctant to disclose his own experiences but he prompts his more vocal sister to talk.

To help overcome the stigma, the Stewarts encourage the children to bring their friends home for regular teen dance parties. However, as the youngsters mature they turn increasingly to more private relationships so that sphere of influence is fading.

Brian's employment did not come without a struggle either. Over the years he has repeatedly demonstrated his aptitude for creative problem-solving and breaking down tasks into manageable bits. He devised a method of drawing using a grid with numbers along the bottom and letters up the side. By dictating to Anne where he wanted the lines to go he designed the renovations to their home.

Although he has created countless jobs, he has been overlooked repeatedly when it came to filling the positions. He and several colleagues, among them the late Frank Rogodzinski, designed Concept Special Business Advisors, which helps disabled people and those with a history of mental illness prepare for the workforce. He has worked there for twenty years.

Pat Sisco

Those with severe cerebral palsy are not the only disabled people to feel the pain of prejudice. Pat Sisco's own parents never acquired a positive understanding of her disability after she had polio as a baby in 1942. The disease affected all her limbs, especially her legs, but the cause wasn't diagnosed until she was two years old. At that time polio was often confused with other ailments.

Her mother was effectively a single mom, left on her own without public social services while her husband went overseas to help fight World War II. However, some of the extended family members living within a thirty-mile radius of their Rock Island home in Quebec's Eastern Townships took an interest in Pat. One welcomed her into her house for several weeks at a time while another periodically took her home to be the taste tester for special cooking.

Another baby was born to the Siscos two and a half years after their first child and for several years Pat felt they were treated similarly. The major difference was that, until the age of twelve, Pat was educated at home by her mother while her sister went to school. She said her mother didn't like to ask for help. However, one incident opened her eyes to the differences in her parents' behaviour toward her.

The family was out driving in the family car when the vehicle began to smoke. Immediately they stopped and pulled Pat's sister to safety but left her sitting in the car, terrified. When Pat asked her mother why they hadn't rescued her as well, her mother told her she would have to understand that her sister's life was more valuable than hers and they would treat any future emergency the same way.

Her parents often went out in the evenings. Before they left they would put Pat to bed and lock the door, leaving her younger sister free to roam the house and have friends over. Pat spent many long hours fearing what would happen to her if the house caught fire or some other emergency arose. She had no telephone or any other way of getting help and the car incident haunted those lonely hours.

When Pat finally got to attend school she was three years behind her peers and one year behind her younger sister but to her, school was respite from home and education was such a privilege that she didn't mind. Her mother, who had only a grade seven education, didn't share her love of learning and in fact resented her oldest daughter's academic proficiency. When at age twenty Pat graduated from high school ahead of her sister, "She was just livid," Pat said.

One evening when Pat was in her teens she asked to stay up to study for a test. Her parents returned late and she became a little testy with them. Her father snapped back that she had better be grateful she had a home, that they should have put her into an institution.

Such hostility toward disabled people is not uncommon, although most people do not acknowledge harbouring these feelings. "Since no one is immune to the fundamental negative bias, including those who are committed to human dignity and respect for others, all of us can be expected to encounter situations in which the conditions for the fundamental negative bias will be overpowering," Beatrice Wright said.[10]

Pat went on to university and got her Master of Arts degree in counselling psychology from McGill University in Montreal. She spent the first three years of her career in that city before moving to a new post at the Society for Crippled Children and Adults in Winnipeg, later the Society for Manitobans with Disabilities. There she eventually became the head of clinical rehabilitation services.

In her more than two decades in Manitoba she saw her mother only three times, twice when her mother visited her and once when she went home. They speak on the phone every few months, Pat said. Her father died in his mid-fifties.

Scapegoating, Anger and Hostility

In her fifteen years as a counsellor at the Society for Manitobans with Disabilities, Pat Sisco annually encountered an average of three out of sixty new clients who said they wanted to kill their disabled children, a rate she finds alarmingly high. In many cases she was able to turn their attitudes around, using the professional understanding she had acquired from her own situation.

Living with Disability

One case where the child died under mysterious circumstances revealed to Pat another feature of many disabled children's lives. They often become the scapegoats for any dysfunctionality in the family. In this case the parents were having marital problems which the mother blamed on the disabled child.

Scapegoating showed up in studies reported by Irwin Katz, R. Glen Hass and Joan Bailey with subjects who were not from minority groups. They showed "that people who unintentionally harm another may denigrate the other as a means of justifying the harm-doing. That is, by reducing the victim's worth, the denigration seems to function as a guilt-reduction mechanism for the harm-doer."

In one study testing reactions to disabled people, subjects delivered what they thought were either painful or low-level noises to either apparently disabled or able-bodied persons while that person was involved in a learning task. The subjects who had delivered the supposedly painful noises to the disabled person rated that person's performance more negatively than the able-bodied person's, substantiating the researchers' hypothesis that "there should be more denigration of a victim who happens to be disabled than of a victim who is not disabled."[11]

Robert and Laura Latimer's public denigration of Tracy's life may have been an example of such scapegoating. Laura may have felt guilt at wishing Tracy dead because her husband said it was when she voiced her wish for Tracy's death that he began to plan the murder.

With such abnormal psychological pressures on disabled people it is easy to see where the difficulty in adjusting to a disability lies. It is less in the disability itself and more in an able-bodied society's distorted perception of limitations and those living with the limitations.

When most people encounter a difficulty they adjust to their new reality and move on. Those who experience divorce, poverty or the death of a loved one go through phases of mourning the loss and then adapt to their new circumstances. Those who don't are seen as aberrant, their inability to adjust unhealthy. One of the residents of Peggy's Cove told CBC *Midday* that, in September 1998 grief counsellors had advised them to seek professional help if their symptoms of shock and grief at the Swissair Flight 111 crash near their community did not abate within a month.

Yet it seems that, if disabled people do come to terms with their reality, their adjustment is seen as unhealthy. Most people expect them to grieve their loss perpetually. They are not supposed to acquire a positive outlook or value their bodies and minds. To do so would be to undervalue the normal body and the appearances and obsessive productivity our society worships.

This expectation surfaces in the frequent disbelieving amazement at the cheerfulness of a disabled person in the face of what is perceived as insurmountable ongoing tragedy. It is also evident in the pervasive attitude that disabled people should do anything to become as normal as possible, with normal appearance taking precedence over normal goals. To Pat Danforth's friends her slow, awkward crutches, which kept her upright and more normal in appearance, were preferable to the wheelchair which to her was the more efficient and comfortable method of accomplishing her transportation goals.

Katz et al. found such distorted expectations coloured perceptions of disabled people's characters.[12] In one experiment four groups of subjects were interviewed by the same person. For two of the groups the interviewer sat in an ordinary chair and appeared able-bodied. For the other two groups she sat in a wheelchair and appeared to be disabled. One group interviewed by the able-bodied person and one group interviewed by the disabled person got a friendly reception. The other two were treated obnoxiously. After the interviewer left, another researcher asked the subjects to voluntarily help their interviewer in a different project on their own time and without pay.

The researchers expected the most help to come from both groups receiving the friendly reception but instead, most was volunteered by those facing either the hostile disabled or the friendly able-bodied interviewer. The researchers concluded the hostility reflected the attitude the subjects expected to find in a disabled person. It substantiated the belief that life with a disability is a dreadful fate, an ongoing tragedy so it evoked a sympathetic response.

When the researchers also tested for anger toward the interviewer, they found that "in the wheelchair condition there were more anger responses when the tester's behavior was friendly as opposed to obnoxious" while the non-disabled tester generated more anger when she was unfriendly.[13]

Such misperceptions form a prison far harder to escape than one made of bricks and bars. Yet many disabled people do escape and adjust. Before those who become disabled as adults can come to terms with their new reality, they must confront these attitudes within themselves. For children disabled at a very young age, their lives are the only ones they have known so to them their disabilities are part of their norm. Their greatest need is parents and other adults willing to creatively and constructively learn about a reality different from their own.

Fitting In

Not all cultures share Canadian views on all disabilities. Jim Derksen, former chair of the Council of Canadians with Disabilities and a member of its national human rights committee, said some societies perceive intellectually disabled citizens as blessed with the special gift of innocence and those with epilepsy to have a direct line to the gods.[14]

However, in our western culture these and all disabilities are perceived as abnormal with the definition of abnormal based on some mythical "normal" construct. The very terms invite the separation of people into the acceptable and the unacceptable.

With all the segregating, dehumanizing messages coming from all around them it is small wonder that disabled people frequently succumb to the messages. There is little acknowledgement of their humanity. Instead, most of their experiences after their disabling event say they are not only damaged goods but less human because one or more parts of their bodies or minds don't work like everyone else's. Often, like Tracy Latimer, they are reduced to mere body parts, their personalities totally overlooked.

Since they cannot do the impossible and walk, see, or hear again, the only way they can gain any social standing at all is to accept the less-valued role assigned to them. Some disabled people try to do the impossible. They try to abandon their wheelchairs as Pat Danforth of Regina did after she broke her back in a car accident outside Calgary in 1970. Her friends cheered her clumsy efforts to walk with crutches and braces. Instinctively they and she knew that remaining vertical was a critical social asset. Although she had been living with a barely perceptible disability since the age of four, it wasn't until she began using a wheelchair, which lowered her head to a child's level, that people began to treat her differently. It did not matter that she was a fully functioning member of her community. She was a wife and mother working outside her home and since 1985 she has been an education and equity advisor with the Saskatchewan Human Rights Commission.

Eric Norman from Gander, Newfoundland, chair of the Council of Canadians with Disabilities and a retired assistant school superintendent, said when he began using a wheelchair in 1983 some of his former colleagues patted him on the head. Georgina Heselton from Regina, a Commerce graduate who worked at management levels for the Saskatchewan government until post polio syndrome forced her retirement in 1987, said she gets similar patronizing pats from total strangers now that she uses her wheelchair in public.

Disabled people trying to fit into their communities will accept their society's norms, even those destructive to them. When Danforth got a job with a disability advocacy organization in Alberta, a wheelchair user on the hiring committee told her, "One of the reasons I got a position was because I looked so normal sitting in a wheelchair."

Visual cues affect a disabled person's social status. Derksen said blind people are often perceived as sensuous while deaf people are seen as suspicious. Generally, however, the less noticeable the disability, the more upright the person, the less disfigured the face and body, the better.

Based on these criteria, every aspect of Tracy Latimer's disabilities invited discrimination and bigotry. She had no visibly redeeming body part. Much of the defence argument for the necessity of killing her rested, not on her pain and suffering, but on disability and "mutilation." Tracy's own mother admitted in court that the disfigurement of the proposed surgery was uppermost in her mind when she wished for "a Jack Kevorkian."

However, visibility isn't the only criterion for valuing disabilities differently than other physical features. The person's ability to live by society's norms is also crucial. Those who break the norms, such as people with learning disabilities or mental illnesses, face devastating discrimination, often just as severe from other disabled people as from the able-bodied population. Disabled people adopt the same norms as everyone else and those who become disabled later in life once were part of "everyone else."

On this front Tracy lost out again. The mental abilities she demonstrated were easily dismissed by her parents and the defence as not worth noting. Robert Latimer has said a three-month-old baby could do things that Tracy couldn't. Some disabled people agreed with that assessment and with Robert Latimer's actions.

The disabling event itself also influences the disabled person's social acceptability. Just as the Victorians divided the poor into the worthy and the unworthy, so disabled people feel ranked by how they became disabled. War veterans and seniors—those perceived to have paid their dues—rank higher than those who became disabled in childhood, in careless accidents or, heaven forbid, from substance abuse or a sexually transmitted disease.

All people notice differences and categorize them accordingly. Without that ability one wouldn't be able to recognize people. Disability is simply another category. However, the values placed on the categories can cause trouble. Grouping people according to wealth, power, mental abilities, talents, skin colour or the current definition of beauty is not the problem in itself. The difficulties arise when these categories are used to disparage or discriminate against the targeted group. By the same token, no one is immune from the effects of such value systems and from the negative results of being "othered" or excluded from the perceived mainstream.

The Simpsons

Although one would expect support to flow freely from caring profes-sions such as education and medicine, that is not necessarily the case. Many innovative doctors, nurses and service professionals are sup-portive and willing to provide necessary care but medical degrees and diplomas do not come with empathy halos so Mike Rosner's and Brian and Anne Stewart's encounters with ignorant doctors and teachers are not unique.

Many disabled people have encountered resistance from profes-sionals when they decided to become parents. Allan and Clare Simpson, both polio survivors and wheelchair users, wanted to adopt a child in the 1970s. "We always thought that we might have our own children but we didn't," Clare said. They went to Children's Aid which handled adop-tions at that time.

As prospective adoptive parents they had attended a group meet-ing and filled out a form indicating their intentions. The form brought the head of adoption and another staff member knocking on their apart-ment door, asking them to change their minds. "I could just feel the bristles on the back of Allan's neck," she said.

"For the most part it was because I was disabled," she said. She felt particularly scrutinized because, as the potential mother, the burden of care was presumed to fall on her. According to Clare, other couples where the male partner was disabled had been allowed to adopt with-out encountering such objections.

However, Children's Aid did agree to let the Simpsons go through the same process as other parents, meeting with a social worker and having an interview. When the agency assigned what Clare called a "very open-minded" social worker to them their prospects improved. "She was a wonderful person," she said.

In October 1979 the Simpsons adopted their first baby, an eleven-day-old girl whom they named Julie. The only stipulation was that they had to have public health follow-up visits for a year instead of only a few months. Five years later in October 1984 they adopted another girl, Katherine, age two weeks.

Clare's upper body strength allowed her to lift the babies into and out of the detachable infant seats the Rehab Engineering department of the Winnipeg Health Sciences Centre had designed for their wheel-chairs. Sometimes Allan, whose strength was more limited than Clare's, lifted the babies by carefully grabbing their sleepers with his teeth but Clare provided their physical care.

With the help of a few other physical adaptations they kept the girls safe and sound. Clare used a harness and leash for a short time during the girls' terrible twos until she was confident they would stay with her.

That brought an unexpected reaction. A strange woman accosted her in a mall saying she didn't like to see a child tied up.

Clare doesn't remember having many problems with her daughters. Like Pat she handled danger by training and communication rather than by running after them. "At a very young age they learned to climb onto our footrests and onto our laps."

Keeping up with the demands of their daughters' social and educational activities brought out more attitudinal barriers. When the oldest daughter, Julie, was enrolled at pre-school Clare, then a stay-at-home mom, wanted to be as much a part of the program as the other mothers but the school had no ramp. At first the school officials said they would simply send a teacher out to get Julie but Clare refused. Volunteering was important to her and the other mothers were expected to do volunteer work. "I think it made it easier for the kids," she said. "I remember doing a lot of advocating so I could take my children to a lot of things."

She also joined a daycare cooperative in the neighbourhood. Clare was essentially doing exposure therapy, helping the teachers and children in the schools get used to her children having both parents in wheelchairs. She encouraged her daughters to bring their friends home, again for exposure therapy as well as for her daughters' social needs. When neighbours started leaving their kids with her she realized she had passed the test and was seen as a responsible, capable parent. But she knew the battle wasn't over. She would always have to prove herself.

Julie's memories of her early school years are typical of any child entering school with her friend for the first time: "Mom and Dad chasin' after us with a camera." What Clare thought might have been an embarrassing moment for her daughter, to Julie wasn't worth remembering. Clare remembers Julie shielding her eyes from the sight of friends and teachers carrying her into the inaccessible building. Julie had a different interpretation. She thought she might have been apprehensive that the men would drop her mother.

At the age of nineteen in 1998 she was a drama student at the University of Manitoba. She is more aware than most young women her age of the needs of disabled people. Clare said Julie has already independently turned down an opportunity to live with friends because the apartment was not accessible and would have kept her parents out. In her university drama productions she had to fight for her parents' right to sit together.

Clare stayed at home until Katherine started grade one and then returned to a career away from home. She is the comptroller at the Council of Canadians with Disabilities. Always sensitive to unspoken signals from the people around her, she has found the body language of Katherine's teachers more questioning than Julie's, possibly because she hasn't been at school as much. She fears the diminished exposure therapy may have made school life more difficult for Katherine than for Julie.

The therapy worked best on the girls' playmates. Julie said her friends thought it was kind of "cool" to have parents on wheels because they could get rides on the backs of the wheelchairs. "I had a whole bunch of friends because they wanted to play with the elevator."

She finds her adoptive parents "definitely interesting." Without them she wouldn't have gotten to "hang out with Brian Mulroney and Rocket Richard." Her father was awarded the Order of Canada in the fall of 1998 when the former Prime Minister was made a Companion of the Order. For the occasion the whole Simpson family got to go to Ottawa.

Julie said she got used to being quizzed about her parents. "I don't remember not being asked questions." They would ask her, "Uh, can I ask…" to which she would mentally reply, "You just did." She credits her father with giving her a sense of humour which helped her bluff her way through queries about polio when in fact she claims to know very little. "I think I was always pretty close."

People assume Clare's children help her a lot. "They're not really helpful at home," she admitted. She blames herself for spoiling the girls because she has been so conscious of the need to keep proving herself.

Cateland Penner

Like the Simpsons, Cateland Penner also encountered strong resistance to her dreams of parenthood. Cateland has a moderate form of Tracy Latimer's type of cerebral palsy. She was born with many of the factors thought to cause cerebral palsy—three months premature, weighing only two pounds, blood incompatibility and her mother had an infection during pregnancy. "Needless to say, they didn't have the greatest predictions for me," she said.

She uses a wheelchair but can speak clearly. Although she has a university degree in education she has not found a teaching position and works at the Cerebral Palsy Association of Manitoba. Her husband, Greg, has mild cerebral palsy.

When she became pregnant, she and Greg were elated. They had waited a long time for this. Because Cateland felt more comfortable with a female obstetrician, she got an appointment with someone recommended by her nurse sister but before she got to the appointment she had to be admitted to emergency for complications not related to her disability. They were to plague her throughout her pregnancy.

When in her fourth month of pregnancy she finally got to the appointment with her obstetrician of choice she wheeled into the office and introduced herself. The startled doctor said, "Quite frankly I wasn't expecting anybody like you. You're not planning to continue this." The doctor effectively refused to accept Cateland as a patient by insisting on an immediate abortion. She thought Cateland would require a lot of care and said she didn't have time for that.

Insulted and outraged at the unprofessional treatment, Cateland returned to the male doctor who had admitted her to emergency. He was as ignorant about cerebral palsy as the other doctor but he was willing to learn from and collaborate with his patient. "He was wonderful," she said. After months in hospital she gave birth to a healthy little girl by cesarean section. The doctor let her try a normal labour but with her weakened state from months of hospitalization and complications he kept it mercifully short.

Caring for their daughter brought a further battle, a different manifestation of the negative bias—smothering, over-helpfulness. For the first six weeks after she came home with the baby she had help, the first three from family and the next three from the Family Centre with the option of having three months but the woman from the centre wouldn't let Cateland touch her own daughter. The exclusion left her feeling inadequate as a mother so she and Greg discussed the situation. Feeling they would not be putting their daughter at risk, they let the woman go.

Cateland gets daily help for getting herself dressed but not for her daughter. "She listens and she's very patient," Cateland said. If at any time they felt their child was at risk she said she wouldn't hesitate to ask for help.

More Ignorance and Prejudice

Mike Rosner also encountered ignorance as well as prejudice in his doctors. His first very general diagnosis didn't say what kind of muscular dystrophy (MD) he had. Duchenne MD was ruled out but that left thirty-nine other possibilities and an uncertain future.

At age ten he was re-diagnosed by a neurologist as having amyatonia congenita. However, at age thirty his progressive muscular weakness led him to do his own research and to the conclusion that he had been misdiagnosed. He consulted a researcher in neuro-muscular diseases who confirmed his suspicions and his own diagnosis.

While the new diagnosis didn't change his prognosis, it did make a difference in planning his life. He has progressive deterioration in muscle strength and mobility. For some, life with this disorder is up and down with plateaus much like those commonly found in multiple sclerosis; for others with this type of MD the down stages are steeper and the deterioration is faster. The diagnosis meant he had to plot the progression himself and more firmly take charge of his own life. In 1998 a neurologist prescribed a drug which brings a temporary boost in strength but also difficult side effects such as increased respiratory secretions and intestinal cramping. However, his love of life is undiminished.

Mike is no more a stranger to negative discrimination in his community than the Stewart family. "Oh, yeah. Where to begin," he said. He attributes some of it to unfamiliarity with disabled people and some to structural influences. He attended a segregated school up to grade six and then moved to an integrated school. Both were outside his neighbourhood.

The physical segregation brought social isolation. Some parts of the integrated school, such as the cafeteria where a lot of student interaction occurs, weren't completely accessible. In his social life he was ever more isolated as he got older and the other kids formed increasingly firm bonds with each other. He couldn't get acquainted with kids either at school or in his neighbourhood. He had to leave when his transportation arrived. Indeed, his whole life runs on other people's schedules. He is on the regular program scheduled by the home care department.

The End of Compassion

The attitude Mike found in some medical professionals is not new. In some cases people have suspected, not merely passive euthanasia or withdrawal of treatment, but active euthanasia which in Canada is fortunately still defined as murder.

Allan Simpson, who headed the Independent Living Resource Centre until his death on Boxing Day 1998, recalled an incident when he had polio in 1953 at the age of fourteen. He was in a hospital ward with other polio patients, one of them a boy of about nine. The boy's parents didn't seem to be coping well with his disablement.

One day the boy developed pneumonia. His parents came to see him. They wept over him. Then nurses bustled in, told the others in the room to be quiet and pulled the curtains around their beds. A succession of nurses came and went beyond the curtains, obviously preparing for something but without any of the usual communications. It was an eerie atmosphere, Allan said. Next came the doctors. When they left, the patients heard the boy's bed being wheeled out.

The nurses pulled back the curtains to reveal the empty spot where the bed had been. When Allan and the others asked what had happened to their roommate they were given to understand that he had died then but they weren't supposed to ask any questions.

Decades later Allan's family had a 1990s version of that incident.

His ninety-two-year-old grandmother was mentally alert and still living independently in her own home when a broken hip forced her to be hospitalized. Within two weeks she developed pneumonia. The doctors tried two kinds of antibiotics, both ineffective.

The doctors called a family conference and tried to persuade Allan and the other members of the family to put a do-not-resuscitate order on her chart. As with Mike Rosner they played up the horrors of CPR— breaking ribs, punctured lungs—although other medical personnel say CPR done properly should not cause serious damage unless the person's bones are very weak.

The other members of the family were soon persuaded but Allan and his wife Clare, both veterans of the disability rights movement, quickly realized that the horror stories about CPR were a smokescreen. The doctors' real intent was to withhold antibiotics. The two of them managed to talk the rest of the family out of accepting the advice, the doctors tried a third antibiotic which worked and three years later his grandmother was still alive and alert, living in a nursing home.

David Martin

David Martin's experience with life-saving technology at age sixteen showed a different attitude more like Cateland Penner's second obstetrician. David is the provincial coordinator for the Manitoba League of Persons with Disabilities. Born in France where his military father had been posted, he too was diagnosed with an MD-type neuro-muscular disorder in infancy.

The military transferred his father back to Ontario where other family members lived. After a few years they moved to Edmonton where David attended a segregated school. Eventually, a doctor recommended that he be placed in the school's residence to avoid triggering his persistent respiratory problems. The problems did not diminish but David did make friends and get into mischief, some even against the law; he and some friends started shoplifting but they quickly straightened out when the school called their parents and threatened to call the police.

When the family moved to Winnipeg David attended a neighbourhood school for the first time. Academically he fared better than in Edmonton because socializing was now more difficult so he focussed instead on his studies. His condition gradually worsened until a crisis sent him to Children's Hospital. In Edmonton he had seen friends die in similar circumstances so he thought his life was over.

However, a doctor involved in the use of the first portable ventilators asked him whether he wanted to live a little longer. David said yes so he was given a tracheotomy and portable ventilator. He said he was the first student with such a device to attend a public school in Winnipeg. Now in his thirties he has a full-time job at the MLPD and has been living on his own since his eight-year relationship with a woman ended.

He is again facing new adjustments to his deteriorating condition such as having his food ground up to make swallowing easier but he does not think he will die in the immediate future. He is prepared for more adjustments and he's looking forward to the rest of his life, however long it may be, no matter what it may bring.

Disability, Medical Intervention and Daily Living Alternatives

David Martin and Mike Rosner's conditions may ultimately be terminal but after all, life is terminal. Even if their conditions bring more life-threatening complications, that doesn't mean their desire for further medical treatment is a refusal to accept their mortality. Like many other people living with degenerative diseases, they have probably left the denial phase of the grieving process long ago. After all, they have faced death many times. David had resigned himself to death at the age of sixteen.

In fact, self-assessments of people like them may be more realistic than their physicians', partly because of the already mentioned negative bias and partly because their bodies do not always conform to the standards on which medical texts are based. Instead, their demand for access to medical treatment is based on the principle of equality. They do not want to be refused treatment because of a double standard founded on ignorance and unrealistic attitudes toward disabled people. To prevent the kind of misinformation prevalent in the Latimer case, disabled people have to turn to medical professionals more as advisors than as decision-makers.

Some disabled people do make unreasonable demands on their doctors. So do some able-bodied people. However, years of being denied options available to others could bring an understandable loss of trust in all physicians along with such extreme reactions as hostility and aggression. Others might prefer to passively resign themselves to their fate, handing all decision-making to their care-givers, as also occurs in the able-bodied population.

To Mike and David the feeding tube Robert and Laura Latimer refused to allow for their daughter is not automatically a frightening first step in prolonging terminal suffering. It and the other surgeries Tracy had and was facing are common procedures which improve the lives of countless children like her. David Martin said he is resigned to the fact that he will probably need one at some point but he sees it as a means of improving and prolonging an already meaningful life.

A Voice Unheard

The Stewarts' foster son Jon has had the same kinds of soft tissue releases Tracy had and Clare Simpson had a spinal fusion much more traumatic than Tracy's. She was only ten and spent fourteen months in a body cast, part of that time even before the surgery.

Nor does intellectual impairment necessarily decree lifelong dependence on family. The group home solution rejected by Robert Latimer is one alternative but not the only one. In 1987 Pat Sisco discovered in her counselling that a number of her disabled clients were depressed and angry. Some are non-verbal and some are intellectually disabled. Most are in wheelchairs. Two have brain damage from car accidents. Others deal with dislocated hips and have special seating to accommodate their bodies. Several have had many surgeries. At the time two were living in institutions, three at home and three in transition housing.

When Pat investigated the cause of their emotional problems she found all eight were feeling stifled by their environments. All they wanted was a normal life so she introduced them to each other and with them started the Qu'Appelle Project.

Now these eight live in their own joint home with some support services. The residents collectively hire and fire staff and train their attendants. They get help with budgeting. A management committee headed by Pat and including non-resident advisors gives them guidance, supports them and helps them live with the consequences of their decisions. "They have all found ways with proper support services to lead fairly normal lives," Pat said.

This success again required a prolonged eight-year struggle on several fronts. Pat and the group had to persuade government to pay for extra services such as budgeting, supports not included in regular attendant care or anything the government hadn't supplied before, although most of the services already existed.

Then the Department of Health and Community Services wanted these residents labeled retarded so they could be sent to the Community Services Department which would have required licensing their home under rules and regulations set by government. "We protested very, very strongly," Pat said. Instead of being called retarded they simply wanted to be recognized as people with learning disabilities. This was to be their home, not a government institution with government regulations. They simply needed a few extra supports.

In the end they won and the government stepped away from its customary rigid categorizing practices. The project is now under the Department of Health which doesn't require licensing. It simply gives the grant and allows the tenants to have complete control over running their own home. "It's been very exciting," Pat said. Since they started the project she hasn't seen these clients in her office for their old problems.

Far from Utopia

While not all people with severe learning disabilities would be able to take on such responsibilities, many now living in group homes and institutions would like an opportunity like this. Even children like Tracy Latimer do not have to be an endless drain on their family's emotional and financial resources as long as their families, their communities and governments support the principles of independent living and equal opportunity. For some, group homes are the best answer but all need the flexible, innovative thinking Pat and her clients brought to a situation that would otherwise have been treated with institutionalization, therapy, maybe even drugs, as though these people were somehow deviant for wanting the same life others take for granted. However, as Laurie Beachell said, Canada is a long way from being an institution-free society.

The greatest disability Tracy Latimer faced was the attitude of her parents and other key people in her life. Her cognitive abilities were indeed less than most children her age. However, in Canada we profess to value our citizens on the basis of citizenship alone, not on IQ scores, physical beauty or strength and we do not determine citizenship on the basis of productivity or any other marketplace values. Otherwise most Canadians would fail the acceptability test at one time or another.

We have understood, at least until the euthanasia debate resurfaced, that all abilities are on a continuum not easily separated into acceptable and unacceptable categories. We have also understood that such social acceptability is not founded on facts but on values. Values acceptable to one group will be unacceptable to another. Pain which to most people is a fact of life and simply to be endured, to others is a curse to be avoided at all cost.

With such a range of opinions on ordinary features of daily human life, anything less than unconditional citizenship rights for all jeopardizes everyone's rights. If pain were to determine a person's eligibility for life, whose definition of pain would rule the day? Suffering is an even more nebulous determinant. And, as has been shown, disability is as much a product of society's attitudes as of the condition itself.

Adopting Robert Latimer's argument that killing is a reasonable alternative to medical intervention for children like Tracy is to start down a dangerous road where all vulnerable people can be classified as worthless and dispensable. Disabled citizens like Pat Sisco, David Martin, Mike Rosner, half the Stewart family, Clare and the late Allan Simpson in Manitoba, Pat Danforth and Georgina Heselton in Saskatchewan, Eric Norman in Newfoundland and countless others across Canada have shown that disability is not the only defining element in their lives.

Nor do even severe limitations have to restrict them to miserable existences filled with nothing but pain and leading to death. They know from experience that Robert Latimer's thinking is dangerous, irrational and unrealistic.

These disabled citizens have started to open the window to fresh thinking on physical and mental limitations. Latimer and his supporters would have Canada slam that window shut again, leaving all vulnerable citizens in the stale, stifling air of the nineteenth and early twentieth centuries. Only with inclusive attitudes that level the playing field between those who define themselves as disabled and those who choose to define themselves as able-bodied will that window remain open.

The greatest agony of disability is exclusion from the community. The experiences of these Canadians backed by research show that it is not physical or mental impairments that silence them. It is the able-bodied majority's refusal to hear them, to acknowledge their abilities that can render them as helpless, voiceless and unheard as Tracy Latimer.

Notes

1. Nancy Weinberg, "Another Perspective," p. 143.
2. Nancy Weinberg, "Another Perspective," p. 153.
3. Beatrice A. Wright, "Attitudes and the Fundamental Negative Bias," p. 8.
4. Beatrice A. Wright, "Attitudes and the Fundamental Negative Bias," p. 16.
5. Michael Oliver and Priscilla Anderson, "Theories of disability in health practice and research."
6. Beatrice A. Wright, "Attitudes and the Fundamental Negative Bias," p. 3.
7. Living Will *Form,* Self-Counsel Press.
8. Brian Stewart, "A Parental Perspective," p. 22.
9. Deborah Stienstra and Patrick Kellerman, "Taking action on the United Nations Standard Rules on Disability," p. 5, 14, 21, 26, 29.
10. Beatrice A. Wright, "Attitudes and the Fundamental Negative Bias," p. 17.
11. Irwin Katz et al., "Attitudinal Ambivalence and Behavior Toward People with Disabilities," p. 49.
12. Irwin Katz et al., "Attitudinal Ambivalence and Behavior Toward People with Disabilities," p. 51-53.
13. Irwin Katz et al., "Attitudinal Ambivalence and Behavior Toward People with Disabilities," p. 53.
14. For more discussion of this, see Benedicte Ingstad and Susan Reynolds, *Disability and Culture.*

Chapter Five

Caring for a Disabled Child

"No, no, no!" Every fibre in Laura Schnellert's body rejected the words from the child development specialist. He had said her precious nine-month-old baby girl, her first-born, would never be able to move her arms or legs. The very negative picture he had painted left her only two options: care for her baby at home or institutionalize her. But she was especially devastated to know she would never hear her daughter call her "Mom."

For the second time since Karen was born Laura went into shock. She drove away with her mother sitting anxiously beside her, her body acting and her mind navigating on their own. She didn't know how she got home.

She knew the diagnosis of cerebral palsy was right. In fact, she had suspected long before she got any medical confirmation that there was something wrong with her little girl. Karen was born with several of the many risk factors for cerebral palsy: low birth weight; blood incompatibility; multiple birth—the other twin had died before birth. Karen stayed in hospital for a month but when she came home her intense screaming made her less than a joy to her parents.

At four months she hadn't appeared to be progressing like her cousin who was almost the same age. Karen seemed limp but their family doctor assured Laura that such delays are normal for premature babies. A month later he was still telling her she was being over-anxious.

She had taken matters into her own hands and gone to a pediatrician whose confirmation of her fears was anything but reassuring. She vaguely heard him tell her he suspected cerebral palsy. "I just went numb," she said. "I don't know how I managed to get home that day." That was the first time she had gone into shock. She had driven down Winnipeg's Portage Avenue with tears streaming down her cheeks.

She had had enough presence of mind to realize that she didn't know what cerebral palsy was so, on her way home, she had stopped at the library for some books on the topic. One book had her daughter's name as its title. It became her bible as she observed her baby, waiting for an appointment with the child development specialist. When the appointment came she was more informed than she had been for the pediatrician but her increased knowledge didn't soften his pessimistic prediction.

Before she left the development specialist's office Karen was referred to other specialists and to the Society for Crippled Children and Adults, as it was then known. All that was just a haze to Laura.

With each appointment she was also the bearer of bad tidings to her husband. Like Robert Latimer, he did not accompany his wife to doctor appointments so each searing message brought the added burden of relaying the news to him.

For weeks she sat in the rocking chair crying. She held her baby and told her, "It's not you I don't want. It's the disability." In time, when the shock wore off, she realized she had enjoyed her daughter before she knew about the diagnosis. Karen hadn't changed so she settled down and began to enjoy her baby again.

The Society for Crippled Children and Adults put Karen on a home therapy program with occupational and physio-therapists and a rehabilitation counsellor. Laura saw progress. She noticed Karen was alert, watching things, recognizing people.

Her husband didn't change. He didn't read the material she brought home and still didn't go with her to appointments. Laura was so optimistic about her observations that she thought, if only he would accompany them to Karen's re-assessment six months later, he would change his attitude. She was sure Karen would "knock their socks off."

She was heading for more disappointment. Instead of a fair evaluation the tests required that Karen pick up objects and put them in a bottle, that she match shapes by moving them. "This made me very angry," Laura said.

The doctor then solemnly told them the tests confirmed a significant developmental delay. Flabbergasted at such a conclusion, Laura demanded to know how he could expect Karen to do what the tests required when he had said she wouldn't be able to move. "I was so angry because the tests were so stupid." Her husband was white as a sheet.

Her relationship with her husband went from bad to worse until she realized she had to choose between him and her child. She based her choice on how well she could cope with their situations. While she knew she couldn't help her husband, she was learning to deal with her daughter's needs so she chose her daughter and when Karen was twenty-three months old they moved out.

"I didn't have a lot of support around that," she said. Some family members said she should put Karen into the institution while others accused her of not being a caring wife.

"We lost friends." Some didn't know what to say. Others said hurtful things or refused to talk about her situation at all. They would ask about her parents and brothers but not about Karen. Some were reluctant to hold Karen. Laura appreciated the ones who were honest enough to say, "We don't understand what you're going through but we're there for you."

Unlike the Latimers who rejected the supports they had, Laura Schnellert took what she was offered. She also went on to fight for her daughter's rights, for the same opportunities parents of able-bodied children take for granted. As she herself learned about her baby's disorder, she tried to educate everybody around her. She tried to expose Karen to friends and family, telling them, "You used to hold her and change her diaper before you knew she had cerebral palsy."

She did more than care for Karen's physical and developmental needs. She found herself becoming a friend as well as a physiotherapist and mother to her daughter. "I enjoyed Karen." Laura had some friends with older children who interacted with her daughter but she admitted, "It was a struggle."

Karen was enrolled in the Society's home program and then the pre-school program. With speech therapy from experts and the help of the other children in the program, she even started associating specific sounds with concepts such as "w" for "water."

When Laura returned to her work as a dental assistant to supplement the income from her ex-husband, Karen went to a daycare in a Presbyterian church basement near the dental office. It was the only one that would accept her. The director had a disabled family member and the staff were willing to learn from the agency how to take care of Karen.

Karen blossomed in daycare. "She just loved all the little kids her age." The noise and stimulation augmented the reading and activities Laura did with her at home and enhanced the abilities she already had. Her most controllable movement is pointing with her index finger although she does have some head control. "We just went from there."

Finding social opportunities for Karen and looking out for her physical needs weren't Laura's only hurdles. School brought major attitudinal barriers. The local school division—the same one that gave the Stewarts difficulties—said they didn't have anything for Karen. They had a segregated school but only for those with developmental delays, not physical disabilities, and the regular schools didn't meet either Karen's physical or developmental needs.

The only other option was the day program at the institution she had rejected earlier. When Karen was only two Laura had left her there for a much needed four-day respite stay. When she returned she found Karen had been sedated and separated from the other children. It was the first time Karen had been apart from her mother and the staff said her crying upset the other children. When Laura picked her up, "Her sparkle was gone."

However, Winnipeg's core area school division had a program at Lord Roberts School which Laura checked out and approved. She enrolled Karen and their local division paid the fees as a special needs transfer. The next year the suburban division said they had a place for her at their own segregated school.

However, Laura didn't like it and sent Karen back to Lord Roberts. This time she had to write to the Manitoba minister of education before the division would pay for the second year. Writing seems to be a necessary skill for parents like her. She found that keeping her own records, not just relying on the school's, helped her deal with the repeated explanations made necessary by staff turnover.

Then her local division outright refused to pay but Laura told them, if Karen was to attend that division, she was to be in a neighbourhood school where she would be with kids from the church daycare, some of whom might still remember her. The division told her she didn't have a choice. She said she did.

Her advocacy for her daughter's education rights intensified with help from the Society for Community Living whose lawyer accompanied her to a meeting with the division's senior administrators. She told them she wanted either the local school with a full teacher aid or Lord Roberts. The superintendent told her it all boils down to money. She pointed out that the division chose to spend money on a gifted-and-talented program for able-bodied children. Laura said she had a gifted child who deserved the same respect and opportunities as those able-bodied children. Finally, her lawyer's threat of a lawsuit got Karen a third year at Lord Roberts.

After all this fighting for basic rights with promises of more struggles for less than full integration, Laura was ready to move to the Lord Roberts area so Karen would fall within the school's catchment area. They were already both becoming part of that community. To qualify for the subsidized accessible apartment near the school she had to quit her dental assistant job and become a stay-at-home mom, a new but enjoyable role. After a year she went back to work. She volunteered at the Cerebral Palsy Association of Manitoba, dealing with parents of newly diagnosed children and her efforts led to a paid position in 1988.

Meanwhile her personal advocacy continued. After six years at Lord Roberts, Karen's friends went to Churchill High School while Karen was expected to head for Grant Park High School. Karen's friends wanted her at Churchill as much as Laura and Karen did but that meant a year's delay while the school was made more accessible. The following year it was still not ready and Karen had to spend several more weeks at the elementary school. When she was finally admitted at the insistence of the Lord Roberts principal, she still couldn't get to all her classrooms or eat in the cafeteria with her friends.

The high school's attitude lingered although, by the time Karen left at age twenty-one, glimmers of enlightenment were appearing. By then the community living class closeted at the back of the school had been relocated to allow more integration and the cafeteria was accessible.

Karen graduated at age eighteen, three years before actually leaving in order to allow her to participate with her friends, although she was still excluded from some parts of the ceremonies. Although Laura had warned the school in February about accessibility, the staff discovered a few days before graduation in June that the church where the graduates would be given their diplomas was inaccessible. Laura resisted the staff's pleas for last minute assistance and insisted they solve the problem themselves. She told them she simply wanted to watch her daughter graduate like the other parents. However, the triumphant "grand march" around the school the following Saturday left Karen alone outside the gym with her teacher aid. The gym was still inaccessible.

Karen now lives with her mother in downtown Winnipeg but she is continues to learn, increasing her vocabulary in a community program at the St. Amant Centre, the institution Laura rejected earlier but which has since changed its approach. Karen is a busy young woman, volunteering at Misericordia Hospital, shopping and having lunch with friends.

And occasionally she calls Laura, "Mo-om!" in the disgusted drawn-out singsong that usually leaves parents sighing in weary exasperation. To Laura that word and her tone of voice are music.

Parenting: Doing the Best You Can with What You Have

In many ways the story of Catherine "Cal" Lambeth and her husband Grant Mitchell parallels Laura's. Cal and Grant met at law school but after one year in practice Cal gave up her career to become a mother. Like Laura she soon noticed something was wrong with her little daughter Samantha but her doctors said nothing. They admitted later that they, too, had suspected something but hadn't wanted to say anything until they were sure what they were facing.

Also like Laura, when she heard the horrifying news that her eight-month-old baby girl would live all her life with disabilities caused by cerebral palsy, she sat in the doctor's office sobbing. She gathered all her baby paraphernalia, clasped little Samantha in her arms and left, the nurse following her to her car.

A Voice Unheard

Like other new mothers she had expected that, if she did all the right things during her pregnancy, she would have the baby of her dreams but in spite of everything Samantha had come two months early and now this.

"It was devastating and I was depressed and angry for about two years after," she said. "I was mean." Her anger made her resent other mothers' ordinary problems. She couldn't understand how they could get upset about their children rummaging through the pots and pans when, as parents, they had so much. She'd snap at Grant for minor things, thinking even as she was doing it that she wasn't really angry at him. She didn't recognize her anger until she had left it behind.

From the beginning she generally understood what cerebral palsy is but she didn't know how the diagnosis would affect her, what it meant for her little daughter. Samantha's ("Sam" to her family) development was to be a long journey of discovery for all of them with few guideposts to tell them when they had ended one phase and were beginning the next. Assistance for parents with disabled children is usually segregated from sources aimed at other parents and this is only one of many isolating experiences inherent in having a child who is different. These parents have to turn to other sources for guidance, such as agencies and self-help groups. As with separate organizations for disabled people themselves, such organizations do assist parents by being specifically geared to their needs but their separateness also sends a powerful message of social separation. Life with disabilities does not "go with the flow" or follow easy recipes, either for disabled persons or their families. It requires flexibility, ingenuity, hard work and tenacity.

Cal and Grant discovered they had coping strength. Both already had long-standing experience with disabilities, enough that they instinctively knew there is more to disabled people's lives than tragedy. During Grant's boyhood, his father was hospitalized for a year with a rare neurological disease that left him walking with the aid of arm canes. Cal's sister is autistic and lived with their mother until the latter's hospitalization and death in 1998. As Grant said, "It's been a lifetime of watching life with a disability." They had enough faith in life to keep going, discovering their own inner resources.

Eventually their family grew to include two more daughters but the isolation intruded whenever Cal took Sam anywhere. She said she often felt conspicuous. Because Sam is a wheelchair user, outings always require planning and forethought for even the simplest of excursions. Cal felt like an outsider because she always needed special considerations. They stood out even in school, although elementary schools seem better prepared than other places for some of these needs.

The alienation also came from other directions such as people's misguided observations. Just as Georgina Heselton's husband was presumed to be a saint for marrying a disabled woman, so parents like Cal and Grant are presumed to be either saints or martyrs because they have a disabled daughter. While Cal sees these statements as attempts to compliment her, she also recognizes another motive. "What they're saying is, my kid's a burden."

To her Sam is not a burden. Sam does require extra care but parents with more than one child realize that each comes with distinct needs. Some are more trying than others and similarly, those with disabilities require care appropriate to their needs. To her this was just a part of life, doing the best with what you have just like with other children.

Parents like Cal refuse to accept sainthood or martyrdom. Nor is this mere modesty. Accepting either role means denigrating their flesh and blood. Their sainthood makes the child's presence a sin; their martyrdom makes the child's life their torture. To Cal, raising Sam is not about disability. It's simply about being a good mother.

Not that she downplays the additional stresses brought by disability. Like Tracy and Karen, Sam has had many surgeries. Sam was the first in Winnipeg to travel to British Columbia for a rhizotomy, which selectively cuts nerves from the spine to areas being pulled out of place by wrong signals coming from a damaged brain. It required months of therapy after which Sam decided not to have any more surgeries.

However, to these parents the surgeries and other medical intervention their children required was simply a fact of life, not a reason to opt out of life. As Grant said, "Pain is a condition of life." He cannot tolerate Latimer's reasoning. They know, if non-disabled people were waiting for painful surgery, no one would consider killing them.

Constant Grieving and Adjustment

Dr. Vicki Strang, assistant professor of nursing at the University of Alberta in Edmonton, empathizes with Cal's early anger and Laura Schnellert's grief. Her oldest daughter, Kathryn, is autistic. Delving into research she has discovered that such anger is common in parents with disabled children. Even though it seems to abate, it tends to recur whenever something like a birthday reminds them of their loss or invites comparison with other parents. It becomes part of a chronic sorrow.

"It's like the grieving cycle," she said. "You don't want to. You block it out but it always happens. You dearly, dearly love this child but the resentment builds." She has no happy memories of her daughter's childhood.

Autism brings its own set of obstacles for parents. When Kathryn was born in 1970 it was seen as the result of poor parenting—affluent but cold, distant parents producing autism in the child. More recent research does not blame the parents. At that time, however, since the pattern didn't fit them they were left with no label. Kathryn was also very high functioning and didn't fit the prevalent autism image of an unresponsive child.

Dr. Strang said she had an "intense drive to have as normal a life as possible for Kathryn" so she can also identify with Laura Schnellert's fight with "the system." Yet without a ready-made category for her daughter, she had difficulty explaining Kathryn's needs to anyone. It was either a long, involved lecture about something even the medical experts didn't know a lot about or trying to pass Kathryn off as a normal child. With the former she felt guilty afterwards wondering, "Did I set the stigma up for her?" If she tried the latter as she did when she enrolled Kathryn in Girl Guides, "I was told in no uncertain terms that I should have told them."

Other stresses of disability come from physical as well as psychological adjustments for the whole family. When one person needs a wheelchair, the house must be modified, a ramp or ramps added. Other family members may have to switch rooms. A multi-leveled home might even force the family to move, which in turn might well lower the selling price if potential buyers smell a "motivated vendor." If no financial assistance is available, purchasing additional aids such as a wheelchair-accessible van or elevator might strain family resources.

If the disabled person is a child, the family's expectations for the child's and their own future have to change. Awareness education and physical adaptations in the home may be relatively simple at first and the family's awareness may grow with the child. However, the impairment of an adult wage earner may bring a drop in income until the person or the work site have adapted to the new circumstances or the person has turned to different work, if that is possible. If income drops the family's needs may not be met, social status will drop and emotional stress will increase.

And these are only a few adjustments for one type of disability. Other impairments would require a host of other adaptations. In an unaccommodating world it is small wonder that disabled people and their families require government and community financial support and constant creativity.

In Dr. Strang's case, family adjustments included trying to give their younger daughter, Liz, as normal a life as possible, too. Dr. Strang and her late husband, Allen, tried to keep the girls in separate schools and recreation activities to prevent unfair competition between them and to shield Liz from the stigma of having a sister whose behaviour often didn't fit in with the crowd. Sometimes Liz resented this intrusion when it meant Kathryn getting involved in something she wanted to do as well. When she got older she understood but little children often don't understand adult reasoning.

For Cal and Grant, finances were fortunately not the consideration they were for Laura Schnellert. However, they faced other common stresses. The neighbourhood, public buildings and businesses, or even doctor's offices and hospitals may not be as accessible as building codes require. These may leave not just the disabled person but the whole family more home-bound than they would prefer and increase cabin fever or resentment at the loss of work or leisure activities. Cal said she feels guilty leaving Sam behind when the rest of the family goes biking. Other children may choose not to participate in family activities but Cal knows that for Sam this isn't a matter of choice.

All parents of disabled children need help in making the life-altering adaptations to raising these children. Unless communities reach out a helping hand and become part of the solution, they become part of the problem. Segregated programs, institutions such as agencies and self-help organizations can play an important role in helping such parents and children through the initial phases. Public financial support is crucial in ensuring that parents have an identifiable support system specifically geared to their needs.

However, these are not the whole solution. Unless segregated solutions retain the ultimate goal of integration, they increase the families' isolation. Relief from the care-giving role through respite programs, for example, provides physical relief. However, if care-givers are still left outside their former social and emotional support systems, if their extended families and friends shun them or refuse to listen to their stories about their disabled children as Laura Schnellert found, then these parents have lost much more than their expectations for their child. They have lost their own place in the community. Without real, meaningful integration at all levels and in all aspects of life, the child's disability becomes the instrument for socially isolating and disabling the parents.

Parents as Attentive Observers

Like Cal and Grant, Laura Schnellert is an assertive parent with the vision and tenacity to see potential where others see only ruin. She was willing to accept her baby as she was, to overcome her own aversion to disability, to explore the world of cerebral palsy despite her own apprehension. Because she was willing to see success where others could see only failure, she was rewarded by victory where others had predicted defeat.

A Voice Unheard

As Karen's mother, Laura opposes Robert Latimer. Although she is the program director of the Cerebral Palsy Association of Manitoba, her views do not speak for the organization, which is split over the case, both at the provincial and national levels. Despite its mandate to protect the welfare of those with this disorder and their families, the association has been conspicuously absent from interventions in Latimer's appeals.

Laura acknowledges what disability self-advocates have been trying to tell all Canadians: that care-givers of disabled people are not the experts on living with a disability. They are experts only on care-giving and therefore cannot speak for their dependents; the Latimers and their lawyer, Mark Brayford, were speaking from their own perspective, not Tracy's. At one of several vigils held by Manitoba groups of disabled advocates in memory of Tracy, Laura said, "I must be an attentive, attuned observer."

She is dedicated to helping her daughter meet her needs which are the same as everyone else's, "to love and be loved, to learn, to share, to grow and to experience." She also understands that Karen has the same right as everyone else "to fall, to fail, to suffer, to cry, to despair. To protect her from these is to keep her from life."

Laura developed this healthy understanding of the needs and rights of all children, able-bodied and disabled, partly from her experiences with Karen and partly from growing up with an older disabled sister. She saw her mother acting as her sister's advocate in hospitals, insisting that her child receive proper care.

Karen's father had a somewhat different background. He, too, had an older disabled sibling but Laura said her former in-laws' reactions to the disability were different from those of her own family. Her brother-in-law was blind and his parents expected Karen's father to be his eyes. The brother's goals—getting a university education, marrying and having children—were greeted with scornful disbelief, even though he proved them wrong each time.

Karen's father hasn't seen her since she was five. His reaction to his daughter contradicts the assumption of some disabled people that simple exposure to disabled people will create a more positive attitude. If the context of the exposure is positive, the attitude is much more likely to shift toward the positive than if the context is negative. Even family members may not be immune to the fundamental negative bias author and psychologist Beatrice Wright mentions, and the bias can seemingly pass from one generation to the next.

Knowing Their Place

Families prejudiced against disability exemplify the attitudes of what Irwin Katz and his co-authors call the "majority group." This group imposes a stigma on those with disabilities who "must know their place, keep their aspirations and achievements at a modest level, and refrain from testing the limits of the acceptance shown them."[1] Although parents like Laura Schnellert help their children challenge those limits without the benefit of first-hand experience, disabled parents like Brian Stewart and Mel Graham have experienced those limits themselves.

Like Karen's uncle, Brian has beaten the odds and far exceeded early limited expectations of his potential. Because of his disability he and his wife Anne can speak to both Robert and Tracy Latimer's situations. They have been foster parents to a succession of about twenty disabled children and Brian himself has cerebral palsy. Taking care of these discarded youngsters is not a mission to them; they didn't ask for the job or look for the children. "They came to us," Brian said. But once in their home they were loved like their own.

From the beginning they demonstrated their understanding of all children's fundamental need for unconditional love and acceptance. They nicknamed their first foster son BW because his name was also Brian. BW was living in a group home for emotionally troubled boys although according to Anne he didn't belong there. His teachers invited Brian to tell them about living with cerebral palsy so they might better help their student. Brian, who was then still single, became a mentor to and advocate for BW. After Brian and Anne got married, BW thought their home would be ideal for him but twice they turned him down.

Then Winnipeg Child and Family Services intervened, asking what it would take for the Stewarts to change their minds. As with all parenting, it meant sacrifice; for Anne it meant closing the daycare she was running in their home and learning to nurture, not only their own first baby, Lucas, but also a teenaged boy dealing with the emotional burden of lifelong rejection.

They worked it out and BW moved in. By then he had been getting into trouble in the group home, taking Brian's car and running it into a brick wall. His one-year stressful stay with them ended when he threatened Anne with a knife and was sent to a detention centre.

However, they did not write him out of their lives even then. They maintained contact with him and when they discovered he was about to be released without any plans for easing his transition to adult living, Brian stepped in again and helped BW get his own apartment while Anne cooked one meal a day for him.

With BW on his own the Stewarts thought they wouldn't accept any more foster children but Child and Family Services had other ideas.

A Voice Unheard

Fourteen-year-old David had spent two years in hospital waiting for a home. He had Duchenne muscular dystrophy and brought them an experience with death. Six years after his arrival, at his wish, he died at his home with the Stewarts instead of in a hospital. He knew when the end was near and medical technology could do no more for him. Anne said they had lots of time to talk so she has no regrets about granting him his dying request.

Little Amy was different. She was born to a twelve-year-old victim of incest and had so many health problems the doctors held no hope for her. She was blind and had to be fed with a tube. When she died at six months of age, Anne reacted differently than she had with David. She tried to resuscitate her because she felt this baby hadn't had a chance at life. They grieved her death as if she had been born to them and as they had grieved for David.

Many of the problems of raising a disabled child are no different from any other youngster. One principle of good parenting for all children is to believe in them even in the face of discouraging evidence. Determining the potential of Jon and Noah, two of the Stewart children with severe cerebral palsy, was hampered by their inability to speak. In his early years no one would have predicted Jon's present successes, Anne said. "I just always assumed he was in there." Their own observations told them he is intellectually equal to other children his age.

However, the Stewarts have had to fight to have others recognize their children's abilities and their rightful place in society. School resistance to meeting Ericka, Jon and Noah's needs brought out their parents' persuasive techniques. One of the Stewarts' goals for all their seven children, able-bodied or disabled, is independent living. While the Stewarts have made a lifelong written commitment to their four permanent foster children, they don't plan to be active primary caregivers all their lives. They recognize the need of all children to live an adult life away from their parental homes.

Like all children, disabled ones need to belong. Both Ericka and Jon have changed their surnames to Stewart even though legally they are like their other foster siblings, permanent wards of Winnipeg Child and Family Services. They are part of the Stewart family and Jon in particular wanted his name to show that he belongs. He wanted to remove the stigma of transience associated with being a foster child.

To the Stewarts the legal arrangement doesn't matter. All seven children have equal status in the family and Eva Marie, the teenaged daughter born to them, said she prefers it that way. Like the rest of the family, she isn't comfortable distinguishing between the children born into and those chosen by the family.

Besides expectations, optimism and equality, other central tenets of the Stewart family creed are creativity, problem solving and tenacity, essential characteristics both for parenting and for adapting to any disability. Brian's spastic cerebral palsy is severe enough that little was expected of him in his early years. His ability to disprove pessimistic predictions for his own future fuel his and Anne's optimism toward the children in their care.

They chuckle ruefully at the memory of him being put into a crafts class for which he was ill suited and in which he had little interest. Brian's slow, awkward gait makes an electric scooter more efficient than long distance walking and his speech can at times be unintelligible to someone unaccustomed to it. Exposure increases understanding and he willingly repeats his statements or has someone translate.

Brian's parents were also role models of support, despite his father's alcoholism and the demands of work or other responsibilities. His mother was a nurse and his father sold shoes at The Bay. "I don't remember them ever saying no," he said.

He spent the elementary grades at the Ellen Douglas School, Winnipeg's now obsolete segregated solution for educating disabled children. When he attended the segregated classes at Grant Park High School he got away from crafts and experienced regular school work with his mother acting as his homework secretary for at least two hours nightly. "It was a major commitment on her part," he said. He went on to get a social services diploma from Brandon University.

Her effort paid off and Brian grew up to become a fully functioning, responsible citizen, moving to independent living before his marriage. He became active in the growing disability rights movement and the formation of the Manitoba League of the Physically Handicapped, the original name of the Manitoba League of Persons with Disabilities. There he met Anne Burt when she drove her disabled mother to the meetings. They got to know each other better when Anne became the League's office secretary for a year in 1977. During that year they became engaged and Anne resigned her post. They married in 1978 and two years later Lucas, the first of their three able-bodied children was born. Shortly thereafter their foster parenting began.

For Mel Graham and his wife Marcy, dealing with their son's blindness was not as traumatic as it generally is for able-bodied parents. Although Marcy is not disabled, she does share the attitudes that come from years of pushing back the boundaries impeding disabled people.

Mel was part of the generations of children with special needs who had to leave home at an early age and grow up away from their families in order to get an education. He was only seven in 1954 when he found that his place as a blind child was the special school in Brantford, Ontario. At the time he lived with his family in Regina. He said he was not permanently scarred by leaving home at such a tender age. However, he did have the benefit of relatives living near the school whom he sometimes visited. Nor did he experience the abuse documented about other institutions for disabled children.

He said specially designed environments have the advantage of being tailored to the needs of that particular disability group. This can be reassuring but it also has its down side. Segregation can create a sub-culture that doesn't fit into the larger community and may even be suspicious of it.

In 1958 his four years at the school ended when he became a subject for an education student's Ph.D. thesis back in Saskatchewan. "I thought I did very well to leave (Brantford) after four years."

While returning home made him a part of a wider community, that experimentation thrust him into a school system unprepared to meet even his basic educational needs. During the first years he had no Braille texts so he was forced to listen to what the other children were doing and then, at home, record his memories with the help of his mother. Those days were very long for an active boy who liked to ride his bike even after he collided with the local butcher driving home from work.

After a few years the Canadian National Institute for the Blind supplied Braille texts for him, but always late, sometimes only after the school year had ended. He frequently had to rely on readers, a system which doesn't take into account the differences between spoken and written language.

Always quick to see the glass as half full, Mel still appreciates those years with their atmosphere of experimentation and discovery. He said the school seemed to feel the need to prove something to the community and the problems his blindness presented often became challenges for group problem-solving involving him, the teachers and the other children. There was none of the segregating atmosphere he still finds in many formal so-called integration programs.

Mel was one of the few disabled people in his generation to get a university education, a BA in English. After testing the waters of computer programming and federal government jobs he met and married Marcy. They had one child, a son, who inherited Mel's visual limitations.

Mel and Marcy saw to it that Neil was not wrenched from home to get an education. Neil attended a local kindergarten but later was bussed to another nearby school with a resource centre. "That's where all the blind kids got dumped," Mel said. The children at the school saw through the fake integration and segregated the blind kids socially.

However, Neil did get good Braille training and he learned to work autonomously. In Mel's opinion, learning Braille is the only way blind children can truly become literate. Computers may read for a blind person but they don't require literacy—the association between the sounds of language and symbols on a page—and reading enhances memory.

Now in his early twenties Neil, like his father, is getting a university education. The 1991 HALS census figures said only 6 percent of disabled people get university degrees; 14 percent of the overall population reach this level (see Table 1). Neil is working toward a Masters degree in computer science at the University of Toronto.

Marcy has been a stay-at-home mom so Mel has always financially supported his family alone. Most disabled people can't find work. Even among university graduates the employment rate is significantly lower than for their able-bodied peers. HALS said just over 67 percent of disabled persons with a university degree were employed, compared to 87 percent of persons without disabilities.[2]

Off and on from the age of fifteen, whenever Mel needed work he turned to CNIB's low paying and "not very challenging" canteens. That occupation and the broom factories, where many Brantford school graduates ended up, substantiate Katz' statement about low expectations for disabled workers. However, to Mel the canteen work was also an opportunity to reconnect with people his age whose experiences were similar to his own.

Mel didn't stay with the canteens. In 1978 he became a communications officer, first with the Saskatchewan Voice of Persons with Disabilities and since 1987 with the Council of Canadians with Disabilities in Winnipeg.

His life straddled a period of huge changes in disabled people's lives when they went from being helpless recipients of services and public charity to standing up for their rights as citizens. And many became parents themselves or already were parents when their disablement occurred. They brought a different vision to parents and disabled people alike.

Disabled parents may face a unique isolation. They may find they don't belong with either able-bodied parents' self-help groups or with disability self-advocates. Because the latter are geared to disabled people taking charge of their own lives, their organizations do not include parents of disabled children. Brian Stewart would like to see something done in that area but so far there has been no response.

Parents like Mel and Marcy Graham don't feel comfortable in self-help groups for able-bodied parents. When they attended a self-help group meeting for parents of blind children, they found they didn't fit in. The other parents were dealing with their own emotional trauma while the Grahams simply wanted to exchange ideas on advocating for their blind son's needs and rights.

When they discovered Neil's disability, Mel said he was shocked at first. He had always expected to have a child with normal vision so he did grieve a little. "I don't know that it lasted very long." He took a day off work and went for a walk and after that he returned to his usual cheerful, optimistic self. He felt some sense of responsibility for his son's blindness because of the obvious genetic link but "it was just part of the package." He had engaged in many happy childhood activities not requiring sight so to him, his son's future didn't seem deprived.

He said Marcy's experience was different. She told him she had fantasized during her pregnancy about colouring with her child and she was disappointed at not being able to engage Neil in the visual activities she associated with happy childhood memories. However, like her husband, she seemed to recover quickly from the initial shock.

They didn't return to the self-help group. Mel said he suggested that they try it again and not let his feelings determine their involvement but Marcy, too, did not relate to the other parents.

Supportive Homes and Communities

Another major source of stress for parents of disabled children are outsiders' attitudes toward the disability. Along with the parents' initial shock comes the shock, inappropriate behaviour and often withdrawal of extended family and friends. These assaults on the family's social ties would tax anyone's endurance. Fortunately Cal and Grant's marriage was strong but many marriages, some already hanging by a thread for reasons other than the disability, often do not survive the added strain.

Cal and Grant encountered both withdrawal and genuine support not only in their own situation but also when they took a public stand on the Latimer case. When Theresa Ducharme first challenged him to action, Grant sent a memo around his office of over fifty lawyers asking who would support the idea. Ten said they would. He has received many supportive calls from lawyers but they feel awkward speaking out, taking an unpopular stand. He said he got a very touching letter from a lawyer whose father has ALS, the same disease Sue Rodriguez had, saying she treasured the continuation of her father's life and she supported Grant.

By the time the Latimer case came along, Cal and Grant had made the initial adjustments to their own situation. Cal was the first to catch the sinister implications of the case, perhaps because in 1993 Sam was thirteen, almost the same age as Tracy. Initially Cal, like Pat Danforth, thought Robert Latimer would be convicted and that would be the end of the story. What really goaded her into action was the public reaction to his crime.

Caring for a Disabled Child

Robert and Laura Latimer were being held up to the Canadian public as the model of long-suffering, self-sacrificing, caring parents. They were accepted as the experts on living with cerebral palsy and on Tracy's life. When depicting the Latimer situation the media invariably consulted those parents of disabled children who sympathized with the Latimers. Those who opposed him were shunned.

Cal and Grant compared this case to Susan Smith in the United States who drowned her two able-bodied sons. "The reaction in the public was so profoundly different," Grant said. He was shocked at the constant comparison made between Tracy Latimer and animals.

Even some of their friends who had known them before Sam was born, spoke sympathetically about the Latimers, then caught themselves adding that, of course, they didn't include Sam in their conclusions about such children. When Grant challenged their statements they would at first justify themselves by pointing out that Sam could talk whereas Tracy couldn't. He would persist, asking whether they would feel differently about Sam if she couldn't talk. Invariably they said no. He said he could usually get them to change their thinking but it took effort each time.

Since Grant is a former prosecutor and defence lawyer now practicing labour law and Cal used to practice law, they were both sensitive to the legal implications of the case. They found the legal arguments an affront to their profession. The case was so far from real necessity that it was "embarrassing" to have someone in their profession put forward such reasoning.

Cal said she does not always know what Sam is thinking even though Sam can communicate her thoughts so, to her, the notion that the Latimers were all-knowing when it came to interpreting Tracy's feelings was absurd. Cal had served on the Manitoba Cerebral Palsy Association board. Now she and Grant were mystified by the silence of the disabled community and the Cerebral Palsy Association in the face of such a blatantly pre-meditated killing of a disabled child obviously not resulting from the usual causes of parental frustration or fatigue.

Laura Schnellert and Grant Mitchell said they have not encountered parents wanting to kill their disabled children. Since 1983 Grant has been the lawyer for the Society for Manitobans with Disabilities, the agency to which his daughter was referred. However, he said he has seen a lot of exhausted parents. Laura said she had seen several so fatigued they were afraid they couldn't go on but she thought those contemplating such extreme measures as murder would probably not turn to a self-help organization like the Cerebral Palsy Association.

Most parents of children with cerebral palsy do not choose the path Robert Latimer did. Instead they want their children to live and will go to extraordinary lengths to make those lives more than a meaningless existence. They see value and potential where others see only damage. They truly love the little ones others shun.

Just a month before his death in 1998, Allan Simpson, executive director of the Independent Living Resource Centre in Winnipeg said, "Every life has a potential regardless of the level of disability."

Like able-bodied children, disabled ones are more likely to thrive in supportive homes than in either nonsupportive environments or institutions. All growing minds and bodies need love and nurturing to reach their potential. As disabled parents of two adopted able-bodied girls, Clare Simpson and her late husband have provided that love and nurturing for their daughters. Like all parents, Clare wants her children to become self-reliant, to become independent in spirit with good self-esteem and have a place where they can contribute to their community in work and service. "Independent to my mind also means to be a contributor," she said.

Grant and Cal want for Sam what they want for their other daughters. "You want them to attain their dreams," Cal said. "Sometimes you see the barriers." And with a disabled child the barriers may be more obvious. When Sam was looking for a career she applied for and was accepted into the education faculty at the University of Manitoba because she wants work involving children. Cal was apprehensive because she saw all the obstacles Sam would have to overcome to fulfill her dream but she didn't interfere. She let Sam discover for herself that perhaps she should look elsewhere to fulfill her goal of working with youngsters.

A Supportive Attitude

If parents of disabled children see nothing but barriers and burden, the result can be perpetual grief, as with Laura Schnellert's husband, severe long-term depression or even destructive behaviour like Robert Latimer's. Pat Sisco encountered some of these parents in her fifteen years of counselling at the agency to which Karen was first referred. Each year about 5 percent of her new clients—three out of sixty—said they wanted to kill their disabled children. Lost in their own despondency they forgot they were speaking to someone as severely disabled as many of the children at the agency.

In one case she had been counselling a mother whose disabled child lived at the St. Amant Centre in Winnipeg. The little girl had an uncertain life expectancy but when she died at home on a weekend visit she was not facing imminent death. Like many such cases, this one was not investigated.

Pat's own parents were more like the Latimers than Laura Schnellert, the Stewarts or Grant Mitchell and Cal Lambeth but, instead of resenting her destructive clients, she tried to help them see their lives from another angle. When she counselled such clients she looked at their backgrounds, their general outlook, their values, what they enjoy, what is important to them. She found that those who had weathered some trauma seemed to have a stronger philosophy of life, a vision of something to hold on to that took them beyond their immediate difficulties. She said the parents with limited, non-challenging life experiences or materialistic values are less able to cope with a disabled child than those with deeper values. Those who can appreciate the things around them can see worth in the life of a disabled child.

For parents having difficulty with their children's disabilities, delving into their values often helped them see alternatives and acquire new understanding. Pat would often tell them she would be able to enjoy life just as much if she were poor as if she were rich. Failing that approach she would simply tell them their child has options and then show them what they were.

Support systems such as respite are crucial, she said. "They've got to know that they've got some supports." If they feel they are giving up their lives to support a child in whose life they see no value, they don't see much point in going on. They see only suffering. By providing care for the disabled person either at home or in an institution to give the care-giver a rest or an opportunity to do other things, respite provides distance which in many cases lets them see their lives differently. In the Latimer case respite was used frequently.

Despite having no children of her own, Pat's work with such parents was not just theoretical. When she still lived with her parents in Québec she became somewhat of a surrogate mother to the youngest two of her three sisters. Babysitting them taught her the fine art of directing children away from harm's way without resorting to strong-arm tactics. Because of her weakened limbs the thrill of the chase was out of the question so she devised other child-rearing methods such as diverting their attention and reading to them. Pat's methods came in handy later when she counselled parents in alternative child-rearing practices.

She, like the Stewarts, the Simpsons and many other disabled people, could understand these situations from both the care-giver's and care-recipient's points of view. However, that understanding does not include condoning murder and Pat sees Tracy's death as murder, not mercy killing. If Robert Latimer is shown greater lenience than other murderers, parents having difficulty accepting their child's disability will be more likely to turn to murder than counselling.

Pat and disabled care-givers like her and able-bodied parents like Laura Schnellert, Cal Lambeth and Grant Mitchell will continue to fight for greater enlightenment among the general population as they fight for their disabled children's rights.

Fighting for their children's public and private rights seems to set these care-givers apart from the Latimers whose lawyer emphasized how much of a burden Tracy was. Parents like Laura Schnellert do not gauge their children's worth by the amount of care they require but by the hopes and dreams they have for them regardless of their limitations.

These parents realize that no children ever live up to their parents' expectations completely. They know if that were the criterion for determining a child's worth, all children would become as disposable as Tracy.

Parenting is tough. Few, if any, can do it effectively alone. All parents of disabled children need support. Some of that assistance exists but as long as it focuses on separation rather than integration, it will never accomplish what most of these parents and their disabled children really want and need—to be a part of, not apart from, their communities.

Notes

1. Irwin Katz, et al., "Attitudinal Ambivalence and Behavior Toward People with Disabilities," p. 52.
2. Statistics Canada, "Health and Activity Limitation Survey" (HALS), pp. xx.

Chapter Six

Another Look

The Latimer case is about much more than murder versus mercy killing. It extends far beyond the Latimer farm at Wilkie, Saskatchewan, to all of Canada. It is about attitudes toward disability and disabled citizens.

Robert Latimer's crime has opened the door to arguments that only a few years ago were unthinkable. When Sue Rodriguez asked for a constitutional exemption so she could have a doctor-assisted suicide, there was no talk of ending someone's life without that person's consent. Robert Latimer widened that discussion to make the murder of a child socially acceptable. He brought a shift in attitudes.

Reversing that shift requires more than simply recognizing the death of Tracy Latimer as murder and not mercy killing. It is not enough to show the cruelty of killing a defenceless, dependent child. It is not enough to demonstrate that disability is not a fate worse than death, that even severely disabled people's lives do not have to be an unending burden on their families and can include all the ingredients most people value: love, family, friends, being part of and contributing to the community. Reversing this shift requires a more open-minded attitude toward disability and a mindful examination of this murder, of possible causes other than Tracy's condition, of Latimer himself and of the implications for everyone of legal and social changes. Without that, this murder will be repeated.

The Line in the Sand

The debate around the Latimer case has been divided primarily into two sides: the pro-Latimer side, which sympathizes with him and/or his views, and the side opposing lenience for him. Judging by formal and informal polling results, most Canadians fall into the first camp while most disabled activists and their supporters are in the second.

The pro-Latimer side accepts motive as significant to the murder, that the motive was mercy, that there were really no humane options, that Tracy was too cognitively impaired to fathom what was being done to her, that the murder was simply a compassionate hastening of an already imminent death. It was just a more complicated version of the Sue Rodriguez story with the father acting as proxy, the role of all good parents with children incapable of making decisions.

A Voice Unheard

A variation on this version espoused even by many who disagree with Latimer's actions was that Tracy's care was too burdensome, although neither Robert nor Laura Latimer ever made this claim. Laura admitted to being fatigued after giving birth to her fourth child and her minor surgery but she did not blame Tracy.

These pro-Latimer opinions were likely based in part on the inaccurate perception of a murderer acting in cold blood out of anger, frustration, impulse or apparent self-interest. For twelve years Latimer had helped care for Tracy, bathing her, rocking her, watching bonfires and hockey with her. If his actions were an expression of prejudice against disabled people, why hadn't he acted sooner? Why had he intervened countless times to keep her alive and happy? The cold-blooded murderer theory didn't fit either the man or the history of his relationship with Tracy and the defence pointed this out in the first trial.

Unlike his daughter, Robert Latimer has a lot in common with ordinary Canadians. While he had at times disregarded the law before he killed Tracy, generally he had led a fairly ordinary life. Tracy had not. His life resonated with other Canadians. Hers did not. He evoked public sympathy because he was perceived to be a burdened care-giver. She evoked public pity because she was perceived as a victim, not of murder, but of her disabilities; she was perceived as his burden.

Nevertheless, these versions were still based on the predominant prejudice about disability, that anyone like Tracy who is severely disabled, in pain and facing painful surgery has no positive future and would therefore want to die. It made sense that a caring father would not be able to stand idly by while his unfortunate child suffered unspeakable tortures at the hands of a well-meaning and powerful but misguided medical profession, able to keep even vegetative bodies alive.

These views depended, not only on facts, but also on exaggeration as observers ignorant of disability issues and experiences put their own spin on the events. RCMP officer Nick Hartle presumed the motive of mercy merely after seeing Tracy's distorted body. Latimer's first lawyer claimed burden as the defence. Mark Brayford, his second lawyer, talked about the amount of care Tracy received but used it to substantiate the claim that her condition would never improve and indeed would likely have worsened. Instead of her successful back surgery and the impending surgery being seen as signs of hope as they would have been for an able-bodied person, they became evidence of her never-ending suffering, and the necessity of killing her.

Tracy couldn't win. She was doomed by her disabilities. The murder of an able-bodied child facing the same number of painful surgeries would have aroused public sympathy for the victim and wrath toward the killer. In Winnipeg Lori McGregor's terminal illness sparked the

Another Look

Loonies for Lori campaign, a public effort to save her life. Except for her illness she was an able-bodied child about Tracy's age. The difference in public sentiment toward Lori and Tracy demonstrates that Tracy's disabilities and not the presumed terminal nature of her condition or constant pain made Tracy's murder acceptable to so many.

The side opposing lenience for Latimer sided with the law. The criminal code makes little provision for the intentions of the accused; one such accommodation is in establishing what the charge will be, first- or second-degree murder or manslaughter. According to legal definitions Latimer had committed first-degree murder but ultimately his charge was reduced to second-degree.

This position argued that the law was paramount and Latimer had to pay the price for his actions. Because the Charter includes disabled people, Tracy's murder had to be treated like any other. Her disabilities should be irrelevant. Using her physical and mental attributes to exonerate the murderer was unconscionable, equivalent to throwing Section 15 of the Charter into the garbage, nullifying disabled people's rights to full protection of the law.

While Robert Latimer has much in common with most Canadians, this of the debate side could also see that he has a lot in common with other murderers. According to Winnipeg lawyer and former prosecutor, Grant Mitchell, most people convicted of murder do not re-offend. The Paul Bernardos are rare. Most murderers are ordinary people until they kill someone and are labeled murderers. However, although many murderers show regret, Robert Latimer has not. His justification for the murder has been supported by so many people that he has had little reason for regret. The story has been told so frequently as a euthanasia morality play that his point of view has become accepted as fact. As Mitchell said, "How often do you see a crime where the chief spokesperson for the victim is the murderer?" Usually the murderer's version is suspect by virtue of his conflict of interest. That has not happened in this case.

While the opposition to lenience focussed on the disability element in the murder, it depended on the law to protect the rights of disabled people. The legalistic approach did not appeal to an emotion-based media dependent on stereotypical images of disability so it did not adequately deal with the other trial going on outside the courthouse, in living rooms and coffee shops. Coupled with the shunning from the media, it failed to educate or change attitudes. Consequently the Canadian public was left bewildered when the higher courts rejected Latimer's appeals.

Neither side of the argument took all the evidence into account. The positions were either black or white. Either Latimer was a villain using his disabled victim's condition to excuse murder or he was an epic hero, taking on the world for the sake of his suffering, dying daughter.

The pro-Latimer side said he meant well. Since Tracy was indeed severely disabled, experiencing pain and heading for painful surgery, the "suffering" and "torture" Latimer used to substantiate his claim of compassion checked out. Therefore his claim of compassion was also true. Their opinion that she was at death's door became further proof that his act was that of a kind, loving father.

After nine and a half hours with the accused, some with Laura Latimer there as well, forensic psychiatrist Dr. Robin Menzies diagnosed Latimer as having a phobia of any medical intervention causing tissue damage. According to Dr. Vivienne Rowan of St. Boniface Hospital's anxiety disorders clinic in Winnipeg, it is a common but very treatable phobia.

Dr. Menzies concluded Latimer had successfully suppressed his fear for Tracy's sake for more than twelve years and, therefore, this fear could not have been a contributing factor in the murder. Latimer's complicated scheming showed he was not impulsive or frustrated, that the pre-meditation constituted sound reasoning.

However, this conclusion did not include all the facts either. Again, other possible explanations were ignored. The psychiatrist's examination used Tracy's medical records to check Latimer's claims about her pain. It ignored the fact that those records would have shown Tracy at her worst. After all, she was being taken to the doctors for specific problems and she did indeed have pain at those times. It also ignored the fact that Latimer helped care for Tracy only when she was free of anything that would trigger his phobic reaction of shaking and sweating. When she was in intensive care, hooked up to tubes and needles, he didn't even visit her, never mind take care of her.

The psychiatric examination also did not include Tracy's daily rides on a bumpy school bus nor did it look at the developmental centre's accounts of her progress nor did it include Laura's positive notes in the communications books. These would have shown that Tracy's life outside medical examination rooms contradicted Robert Latimer's contention that she was in constant pain, that the surgery held no hope for her, that her future was bleak. Menzies also did not look at the feeding tube issue and how this device is helping most children like Tracy live to at least the age of thirty.

However, without the fundamental negative bias a different picture can emerge. A careful consideration demands a different scenario, perhaps like the one below.

A Third Scenario

Since neither Latimer's supporters nor his opponents views are adequate to explain this murder, a third scenario is necessary. Such a reinterpretation requires looking beyond the victim's physical condition to include the state of mind of the murderer, the Latimer family and the circumstances in which they found themselves at that time.

Until October 24, 1993 Robert Latimer, known as Bob to his family and friends, was a typical Saskatchewan farmer, ordinary enough not to stick out in a crowd. He ran a grain farm and in his spare time socialized with family and friends, watched hockey on TV or played baseball. With the exception of Tracy, his family was equally ordinary. His wife was a busy stay-at-home farm wife and mom, assuming most of the child care, meal preparation and housework. She was as active in the community as her home duties allowed.

Before marriage Robert Latimer had several run-ins with the police and minor convictions for drunk driving and possession of drugs. However, when he met and married Laura he settled down to a typical farm life.

He was deathly afraid of needles and anything causing tissue damage. In grade five he had run screaming down the school corridor after a vaccination. His sister testified that in grade nine he fainted on another such occasion She also said his siblings had teased him about his fear on visits to the dentist. He became quite successful at avoiding anything that brought on the sweating and shaking he told Dr. Menzies about. Laura testified he had been relieved that getting married in British Columbia allowed him to avoid the blood test mandatory elsewhere.

Dr. Menzies testified that such phobias tend to run in families and Latimer's family fit the profile. His mother, a teacher, also couldn't stand the sight of injuries. Although the fear clearly did cause some disagreement between Robert and Laura at times, ordinarily it didn't seem to interfere with their lives. One disagreement came with vaccinations. Latimer thought they were "cruelty" and, if he had been the one responsible for taking the children for their needles, they wouldn't have been immunized, Laura said on the stand.

He could not be in the delivery room with Laura when she gave birth. He would take her to the hospital and then, like fathers in the olden days, wait for everything to be cleaned up before he would see her and his new child. Otherwise he usually avoided situations that brought on the phobic reaction. When his sister, a nurse, came to visit and started to talk about her work, she had to stop and wait until he left the room. He did not visit friends or family in hospital, including Tracy, if they had intravenous needles in their arms. If he unexpectedly came across something he couldn't handle, he used avoidance strategies as his sister noticed when he turned over a magazine with a picture of a syringe on the cover. Usually he left doctor visits to Laura, even Tracy's regular appointments. On those rare occasions when he did go along, he studiously avoided looking at anything in the doctor's office that would spark the fearful reaction.

After Tracy's seizures were controlled, things settled into a routine and the Latimers decided to have more children. About three years after Tracy's birth, Brian came along and in another two years, Lindsay.

Robert Latimer obviously got used to Tracy's stiff little body. He held her, rocked her, bathed her and allowed her to teasingly pull off his glasses, throw them on the floor and turn back for his mock scolding. Tracy's surgeries were another matter. He never got used to the needles or the "cutting" surgery and, judging by Dr. Menzies' testimony and Bob's unwillingness to acknowledge the fear, it embarrassed him.

Apparently Laura didn't question his refusal to allow a feeding tube for Tracy even though she had less trouble facing such procedures than he did. In their 1997 CBC TV interview with Hana Gartner he repeatedly and vehemently denounced feeding tubes, "cutting" and "sawing" while Laura's focus was proportionately more on pain. Because this was in a taped interview, editing could have been a factor. However, his increased agitation while talking about anything that would be part of his phobia would support the conclusion that the emphasis on cutting and feeding tubes was not created by CBC editors.

The feeding tube decision was also influenced by inadequate information. Robert's sister told him and Laura that medical people see feeding tubes as just the first step in prolonging a dying patient's suffering. There was no evidence in court that anyone told them feeding tubes are helping other children like Tracy live longer, more comfortably, develop to their potential and maybe even ease the burden on the care-giver. Judging by this misinformation and their decision to reject tube-feeding, to them Tracy was dying anyway. There was no evidence presented in court that the doctors questioned their decision; the Latimers didn't receive counselling in coming to their conclusion so no doubt they thought it was the right thing to do even if it meant letting their little girl slowly die of starvation.

Maybe it didn't occur to them that they were letting Tracy starve; Laura's trial testimonies suggest they turned the situation around to blame her condition. It wasn't they who were refusing to feed her in the only possible way she could receive enough nourishment; it was she who couldn't eat enough or keep enough food down.

Tracy recovered her eating ability after the doctor changed her medication. She didn't die, but she didn't grow and thrive like their other children either. With every surgery there were improvements but her growing body always brought other problems, many possibly exacerbated by her malnutrition. Tracy's body became more and more twisted, pulling her head back until it was hard for her to swallow. Laura usually fed her. Children like Tracy are extremely sensitive to strange stimuli so it was best to have the same person consistently feeding her.

In 1991 Laura had a miscarriage which everyone blamed on the burden of caring for Tracy. The Latimers clearly wanted another child. If they hadn't, Laura would have had the tubal ligation before she could become pregnant again. They had obviously discussed the likelihood of Tracy's death during the feeding tube crisis.

In the event that Tracy lived long enough to require more care than they could provide, Laura had been involved in getting a group home in Wilkie where they could put her. They didn't expect Tracy to learn much. As Laura said to the court, she talked to Tracy but Tracy couldn't talk. To Laura, communication meant talking even though she was clearly aware of and responded to Tracy's body language, such as signalling that she was full by pretending to be asleep.

Then in 1992 Tracy had to have surgery to straighten her back and hopefully improve her eating and prevent damage to her hips. The procedure would involve attaching two stainless steel rods to either side of her spine. The procedure would be very painful and then there were always the seizures she had had since birth. They had been brought under control to the doctors' satisfaction but the medication to control them made pain management more difficult. However, Dr. Dzus' testimony suggested Tracy's pain was under control as long as she was in hospital and Laura's journal entries showed that Tracy's pain at home was under control enough to let her travel daily on a school bus.

Laura told the court that, as she washed Tracy with the staining antiseptic solution the night before the surgery, she dreaded facing her daughter afterwards. Tracy was so innocent and didn't know what she was facing. How could her mother warn her, help her prepare herself?

Robert dreaded the surgery as well. Although this is normal behaviour for parents who see their children being hurt, even for caring reasons, undoubtedly the phobia would have been part of his reaction. He said to Hana Gartner years later that if he felt that way, what was Tracy feeling? She was the one actually going through the operation. Was Latimer projecting his own feelings onto Tracy?

She recovered more quickly than most children and could eat better than before. Laura became pregnant again and this time they used respite services more than they had before the miscarriage. Respite was already a familiar option. They had used the local hospital's respite services before the group home was built. Tracy had been in the Wilkie group home several times for short periods even before she went to the one in North Battleford.

She was doing so well after the back surgery. With the few exceptions when a move made her cry out in pain, she needed repositioning or she regurgitated her food, she was all smiles, playing with the bells and toys attached to her wheelchair and she wasn't as much work as she had been.

From November 1992 the doctor had been talking about more surgery in a year. The hip was starting to go out of joint after all but it wasn't causing major problems. Even in the spring of 1993 before she went to North Battleford for three months, her father could still massage it back into place after giving her a relaxing warm bath.

In early July 1993 Tracy went to the group home in North Battleford, instead of the one in Wilkie which was full. The home hired an extra staff person to accommodate Tracy's care and everything seemed to be going well. The Latimers visited her there regularly and Robert would hold and rock her.

In mid-August baby Lee was born. By then Laura, Robert and the children could well have adjusted to life without Tracy. Laura's application for an extension of her daughter's stay at the home showed that although she had coped before with caring for a newborn in addition to Tracy, somehow this time it was different. By this time Tracy was almost as tall as she. She asked for and got Tracy's stay extended to the beginning of October.

At the end of August Laura applied to have Tracy placed permanently in the home. She didn't talk it over with her husband beforehand. Although she probably anticipated his objections, she was going to have a tubal ligation in early October and she was already tired. She submitted the application.

Sure enough, when the worker came to the farm in September to discuss the application, Robert resisted her decision and, as usual, she gave in. Evidence at the trials suggests that she invariably deferred to his wishes.

On October 3 Tracy came home. The next day she was back on the school bus headed for the developmental centre to show off the ribbons she had won in bowling. Tracy went back to the group home from October 8 to October 11 while Laura had her minor surgery.

The news Laura got from Dr. Dzus on October 12 was the last straw for her. Not only was the hip worse but it probably could no longer be salvaged. Instead of a reconstruction, the top of the thigh bone would likely be cut off, leaving Tracy with one limp leg and one stiff one.

The news couldn't have come at a worse time for Laura. She hadn't adjusted to having Tracy back home, to taking care of two completely dependent and two school-aged children. She was still slightly weakened by her own surgery and Robert wasn't as helpful as usual because it was harvest and, as grain farmers do, he worked from early morning to late in the evening, until night dew made the grain clog up the combine.

Laura told the court that she broke down in the doctor's office but she managed to collect herself enough to drive the 200 km. back home. She got supper and took care of the children. When she and Bob were in bed, finally alone, she told him what the doctor had said. They cried together. Laura confided that she wished she could call a "Dr. Jack Kevorkian" to end Tracy's misery.

As Dr. Menzies testified in the second trial, Robert didn't say anything. He rolled over and pretended to sleep. However, he was far from sleep. He decided that night to kill Tracy. From that day until Tuesday, October 19 he considered different methods of carrying out his plan as he sat alone on the combine, harvesting his crop—a good one that year. What method should he use? A gun? Drugs?

Exhaust fumes. The perfect solution. Easily available. Easily harnessed. Robert would have known that farmers had a long-standing tradition of gassing rodents and unwanted animals back in the days of wooden granaries. As several witnesses said in court, lots of people died or came close to dying accidentally with carbon monoxide poisoning when their furnaces or chimneys malfunctioned and most didn't even realize they were dying. He had everything he needed.

Latimer's choice of method is understandable in his circumstances. Tracy wouldn't have been able to swallow enough to kill her and he wouldn't have considered an intravenous method even if he had had access to such equipment; it would have involved the very apparatus he feared so much. And exhaust wouldn't make any holes in Tracy's body the way a gun would.

The note to the developmental centre on that day, October 19, was the last in Tracy's communications books. Five days later Robert Latimer carried out his plan and carefully placed Tracy's limp body back in her bed in a sleeping position. He was so single-minded in his plotting that he did not think about his oldest son who shared a room with Tracy. He did not consider what a ten-year-old boy like Brian might feel if he were to discover his sister's dead body, as he easily could have. In 1997 Robert told Hana Gartner he hadn't considered the other children. He also said they would not have to watch Tracy have any more operations.

He saw no reason why anyone else should question his conclusions. As he showed by his absence of remorse and his later attempts to justify burning evidence, he just didn't want to answer any questions.

Dr. Menzies called him stubborn. Clearly, in his home his word reigned supreme and he didn't put his actions in the same category as other murders. He told police Tracy had died in her sleep.

Latimer was unhappy with his first lawyer, Richard Gibbons, who said motive could not be considered in a murder case. Latimer was much more satisfied with Mark Brayford who assured him that, although technically motive was not supposed to be a factor in determining guilt, juries had been known to take it into consideration anyway. By the end of November Latimer had switched from Gibbons to Brayford.

Unlike Susan Smith who was photographed stooped under the weight of public condemnation for drowning her able-bodied sons and lying about it, the photos of Robert Latimer always showed him walking upright, smiling and unrepentant. Why shouldn't he? Hardly anybody was totally condemning him for killing Tracy. Many were actually commending him! His family, friends and neighbours were rallying around him, taking up a collection for his legal expenses. Even the police had been sympathetic to him as soon as they saw Tracy's twisted body.

Soon he and Laura were invited to tell their story on CBC TV in Saskatoon. He wasn't being treated like a horrible criminal. There is some evidence that Latimer had become media-savvy. He knew just how to modulate his voice and mannerisms to evoke maximum sympathy from his audiences. In the editorial "Victims of the Latimer Case" in the September 1998 issue of *Canadian Lawyer,* executive editor D. Michael Fitz-James described Latimer preparing for a television interview at his farm. Fitz-James watched the satellite feed monitor for five minutes before the interview began. When it started he noticed, "What a change. Latimer's voice dropped several octaves to a sad and quavering monotone. The boisterous guffawing person of a few seconds before was now downcast, with furrowed brow talking about his late daughter's perpetual pain, his pain, the injustice of it all."[1]

Monster or Care-Giver?

This scenario removes the sainthood that has been bestowed on Robert Latimer. However, despite the horror of his action, this scenario does not reveal a monster. Instead, it reveals an ordinary man with some fine qualities and some that are less than heroic.

The above slightly speculative version of events shows how a number of factors inside and outside the Latimer home could have converged, culminating in the murder: a new baby; Tracy's return after an extended respite period when in all probability she was no longer part of the family's daily routines; the harvest leaving Laura with more of Tracy's care; Tracy's dislocated hip and the threat of an unanticipated type of surgery; Laura's tubal ligation and another brief period without

Tracy. Childbirth, minor surgery and the extra work probably made Laura feel more fatigued than she ever had before.

Robert Latimer added to his wife's stress by stubbornly overriding her wish to place Tracy permanently in the group home. The public focus on Kevorkian and Rodriguez may well have created the impression that Tracy's situation fit the criteria for assisted suicide or euthanasia. Latimer's refusal to seek treatment for his fear left him dependent on Laura's assessment of Tracy's situation and Laura's assessment was distorted by her fatigue.

Only a few of these stresses were directly associated with Tracy's care; most had nothing to do with her pain or the impending surgery. Probably none of these factors on its own would have sparked a reaction as extreme as murder but occurring simultaneously they could have. The timing of Latimer's decision and his constant carping about cutting and force-feeding suggest that his own fear influenced him more than Tracy's intermittent pain.

However, these factors do not excuse him from a murder conviction. Burden is not an escape hatch for him; Laura Latimer was the one who bore most of the burden of Tracy's care and it was she whose stress levels were most affected during the time leading up to the murder.

Then, too, most parents do not wish their disabled children dead. Although the Latimers took care of Tracy for almost thirteen years, they did not develop positive attitudes about her as Laura Schnellert did about her daughter. They definitely had a negative attitude about disability that prevented them from seeing Tracy as a person. The thought of ending Tracy's life was the result of their fundamental negative bias about disabilities and Tracy. According to Laura's testimonies she saw nothing in her oldest child but deficiencies and dependence; she saw no hope, no future. Like her husband and sister-in-law, she did not view the refusal of tube-feeding as depriving Tracy of the necessities of life.

It would surely not have occurred to Latimer to kill Brian, Lindsay or Lee just because they had had several surgeries and were scheduled for more—unless, of course, they were disabled like Tracy. Their bias let both of them rationalize that Robert Latimer had done a great service for Tracy, that he had acted out of compassion.

His aversion to the group home option may also have been rooted in the feeding tube issue. In Tracy's physical state he may have feared pressure from the staff to have a tube inserted or to explain why he was so opposed to it.

Robert Latimer is probably as good a father, husband, farmer and community member as most other men but that is not the issue. It does not matter how wonderful a man Latimer may be in all other aspects of his life. He killed his daughter. The issue is not Robert Latimer's character or status; the issue is murder. While he claims to have done it out of compassion, the evidence does not support this defence. The murder of Tracy Latimer cannot be called mercy killing.

Acknowledging that Latimer must spend at least ten years in prison does not preclude acknowledging the caring side of his character or losing sympathy for him. Putting an otherwise decent citizen behind bars for a decade may seem excessive because the man's image doesn't fit the stereotype of the hardened criminal. To those who see only his positive characteristics, it would be hard to believe this caring person who bathed and rocked his daughter, could be so evil as to warrant such a long sentence.

Norman Kunc, Canadian consultant and speaker on education, disability and social justice issues, separates caring from competence. "Many human service professionals assume that because they care for people their actions are inevitably competent. As soon as you challenge the competence of their actions, you're seen as questioning their caring for the person."[2]

By separating caring from competence, it is possible to say that Robert Latimer was both a caring father and guilty of murder. The fact that he cared for Tracy's physical needs and rocked her does not mean he was a competent care-giver when he killed her. He may have rationalized that he was looking out for her but that doesn't mean he actually was or that he had the right to ignore the law against murder.

He also should not have the right to avoid the consequences of his actions as defined by Canadian criminal law. Justice must be done and be seen to be done for both Tracy and Robert Latimer. It must use existing laws without bending or changing them for no good reason to accommodate this one criminal or ignore this one victim.

Justice for Robert Latimer

In the case of Robert Latimer the law must be enforced as it would have been had his victim been able-bodied. Robert Latimer is neither a demon not a hero, he is just an ordinary human being, complex and frail, making life-and-death decisions in a stressful situation. Robert Latimer may have genuinely believed he was making the right decision for his daughter. The pain she would have been in from her various surgeries, the disappointment he and Laura felt when those surgeries had not brought about the expected improvements for Tracy and his fear of a future which would see more surgery may have been exaggerated by his own fears and distrust of medicine and hospitals. His belief in the rightness of his decision to end Tracy's life may have been succored, as well, by the public sentiment for Sue Rodriguez's plea for autonomy and for Jack Kevorkian's crusade for assisted suicide. Nonetheless, he committed murder, he made a very bad decision. Confessing was not enough.

His decision wronged Tracy; his decision jeopardized safeguards protecting other disabled Canadians; he wronged society. This was not merely an internal family matter. The Charter guarantees disabled people equal protections under the law. To give Robert Latimer special leniency by granting him a constitutional exemption is to set a terrifying and regressive legal precedent. The Charter rights of disabled people must be respected. In this way, the verdict and sentence in this case is the measure not just of justice for Robert Latimer, but also of the legal protection of disabled Canadians.

Robert Latimer has the right to and has been given due process of law. Twice he has been tried and convicted of second-degree murder. Twice he has been granted appeals to the Saskatchewan Court of Appeal and now to the Supreme Court of Canada, where the government of Saskatchewan's appeal of his sentence will be heard in the fall of 1999. This final appeal should be accepted. He must serve the prescribed time. The laws as they now stand do apply to him and they must be enforced. Otherwise his actions jeopardize other Canadians.

The facts do not support the defence of necessity, that because of her alleged constant, increasing pain and suffering, letting Tracy live would have been a greater evil than killing her. Justice Wimmer did not realize that her pain was not constant but he did recognize that it was treatable; Robert Latimer, by murdering the patient, rejected the available treatment of surgery. Wimmer rejected the argument.

Nor do the facts support the defence of mercy killing being used outside the courtroom. If Tracy's pain was as great and as constant as the Latimers claim, the daily ride on a school bus would have been unbearable.

The convergence of factors in the Latimer home suggests another view, one which does not give Latimer reprieve from jail. His phobia confirms that the causes he gave for his actions, while a significant part of a complex situation, were likely exaggerated by his own fear.

The conclusion that his phobia was irrelevant was based primarily on the word of Dr. Menzies. However, Menzies was not trained in phobias—a necessity, according to Dr. Rowan of the St. Boniface Hospital anxiety disorders clinic—and he considered only the negative aspects of Tracy's life. This shows an ignorance of disability issues. Therefore, his conclusion about the irrelevance of Latimer's phobia is, at the very least, questionable.

If Tracy's pain was magnified by her father's fears, and if these precluded treatment for that pain, one must ask why the Latimers have become the primary spokespeople in establishing the victim's level of suffering. Latimer's supporters have to acknowledge that the source on which they have built their case for euthanasia and lenience is invalid.

In seeing such a link, some may be led to argue that Robert Latimer's guilt is mitigated by insanity. All the evidence suggests, on the contrary, not only that Latimer himself would reject such a plea but also that such a plea is not warranted. His fears may have influenced his thinking but he was clear about his decision and that it was a decision not condoned by law. His fears do not absolve him of responsibility. He must deal with the consequences and the causes of his accretions. Absolving him of responsibility without forcing him to deal with the causes of his actions would tell him he has been right all along, that he does not have to change his thinking, that Canada agrees with him.

Acknowledging the probable impact of his fear on the events does imply a need for greater understanding of how care-givers' emotions and attitudes can affect the quality of care they provide. Such an understanding means that counsellors and other professionals must be sensitive to a disabled child's entire environment. Robert Latimer's fear and decision to kill his daughter should sound a warning to support professionals of the dire need to be aware of the emotional well-being of the parents of disabled children. It also means that we, as a society, must ensure that such support services are adequate to the task of providing all-around and on-going support to parents of disabled children in order to prevent a similar tragedy from occurring.

Yet, even with every conceivable support, people like Robert Latimer may refuse assistance offered to them, preferring their own extreme solutions to a problem they perceive as insurmountable. Because of that possibility the law may be the only protection disabled children have from parents contemplating murder. It may be the only influence forcing such parents to seek counselling instead of obeying the impulse. But such influence can only be achieved by enforcing the law, especially in a case as blatant as this.

Retaining the law classifying euthanasia as murder would help ensure the safety of disabled dependents. If Robert Latimer is granted an unprecedented constitutional exemption on the grounds he has given, other parents have indicated that they plan to follow his example; after all, the Latimers have already received phone calls soliciting their advice. For parents who turn to people like Latimer to legitimize their negative feelings about their own disabled children, a law that defines euthanasia as murder and is enforced as such would likely affect their actions.

This case will also be used, not only in other similar legal battles, but also to set policies for care-giving institutions such as hospitals and nursing homes. If Latimer's crime is treated like other murders, institutions and professional care-givers turning to the law for guidance would have a harder time defending the kind of treatment Mike Rosner received. Also, able-bodied counsellors who might themselves have a bias against disability would be encouraged to steer clear of subtle pro-euthanasia messages in dealing with their clients, especially those who think like the Latimers. As a result disabled people's lives would be more protected, both at home and in institutions.

Rejecting assistance should never become an excuse for murder. Parents resorting to murder must be held as accountable as any killer of an able-bodied citizen.

The reasons given by Justice Ted Noble, that this is an isolated case of mercy killing and that a constitutional exemption for Latimer won't affect other disabled people, cannot be accepted. This is not an isolated case. Although such parents are by far the minority, an incident like this could happen again and spokespeople for the Council of Canadians with Disabilities say it already has. They point to Ryan Wilkieson and several other instances where parents have killed their disabled offspring. In Ryan's case, his mother used exhaust fumes but chose to die with her son.

Pat Sisco's experiences as a counsellor at the Society for Manitobans with Disabilities confirmed CCD's anecdotal evidence. Annually in her fifteen years of counselling, 5 percent of her new clients expressed a desire to kill their disabled children. She knows that the Latimer case, while it represents a minority, is not an isolated one. If it is treated as such, other disabled dependents will be put in danger. Some may already have been.

As well, to say that Robert Latimer should be treated leniently because he is not a threat to society, that he won't kill again, misrepresents most homicides. We know that most killers know their victims well, that they kill in intimate circumstances, that they won't kill again. On these grounds, Robert Latimer must face the consequences of his decision like all others found guilty of murder.

The phobia connection provides additional evidence that this case does not support legalizing assisted suicide and euthanasia. Using it for that cause would only magnify the wrong Latimer has done. Changes to Canadian law are ill founded if based on the views of able-bodied care-givers with distorted views but not including those of well-informed care-recipients. His views, which quite possibly are shaped by his phobia, are not unlike those arising from the perpetual grief of other able-bodied parents who read their own feelings into their dependents. Such views encoded into law would jeopardize disabled care-recipients. The law must consider the potential victims.

Latimer and his supporters were blind to anything but the victim's disabilities. They saw help for Tracy as torture. They saw the murderer as the victim. They saw justice as injustice. This inversion shows the futility of safeguards if euthanasia and assisted suicide were to be legalized. Therefore, this case not only doesn't support legalizing euthanasia; it does exactly the opposite.

Robert Latimer is not a hero. He is an ordinary farmer with a common fear who decided to end his problem by ending what he perceived to be the source of the problem. In doing that he became a criminal. Unless he and other Canadians recognize this he will never get the help he needs. To make him into an advocate is to make his thinking a model for all parents with similar attitudes in similar situations. That would make Robert Latimer into one of the most dangerous people in Canada.

Protecting Latimer from the just consequences of his actions discriminates against disabled people by creating a two-tiered justice system: one for able-bodied Canadians and one for those with disabilities. That nullifies justice.

Latimer's justice must involve recognizing that he committed premeditated murder, that he was misinterpreting Tracy's level of pain, that this was not a mercy killing. He must recognize the wrong he has done to society and pay the price Canadian law has put on murder.

Justice for Tracy Latimer

Justice for Tracy involves much more than rehabilitating her father and making him pay his debt to society. It involves rehabilitating the widespread negative bias about disability that made him seem the victim, and to some people even a folk hero advocate for euthanasia. It forces us to address why it was so easy to take a murder and turn it into a case of euthanasia, to reduce the victim to nothing more than a collection of disabilities and ignore her humanity.

Eliminating this negative bias pervasive enough to be the norm is as monumental a task as eradicating racism. Canadians generally agree that prejudice is wrong. Yet it is hard to erase. Just because most citizens agree they should all have equal rights and opportunities doesn't make equality magically materialize or prejudice disappear.

As Mel Graham said, when attitudes change barriers fall. When prejudiced eyes look at disability they see only barriers but when they look at life from a new perspective, unscalable mountains shrink to molehills. Prejudice is based on the human ability to categorize.[3]

In order to fight prejudice, Norman Kunc advocates "the depth of thought." He tells teachers and therapists to keep a journal about their students, and not depend on formulae to guide their interactions.

Increased mindfulness[4] begins with acknowledging the existence of the bias. Combating prejudice involves putting disabled people into context, seeing their abilities as well as their disabilities. Georgina Heselton's abilities were apparent to her immediate family, her husband and her employers. The Simpsons' parenting abilities were obvious to those who chose to see them. Brian Stewart's employable skills made him the family breadwinner. Jon Stewart and all his siblings have potential as do the people in Pat Sisco's Qu'Appelle Project. So did Tracy Latimer.

Mindfulness can also be increased by focusing on the similarities between disabled people and the rest of the population. Tracy needed intellectual and social nourishment just as much as other children, not just physical care and medical treatment. Children like Tracy need the optimism and respect shown in the tenacious ingenuity and love of care-givers like the Stewarts. These children require the creative vision demonstrated by Pat Sisco and her former clients, by the organizations of disabled people and by able-bodied parents like Laura Schnellert, Cal Lambeth and Grant Mitchell.

A mindful approach to the Latimer case also means recognizing differences such as those between Tracy's experiences and those of her care-givers. She never had an able-bodied existence so she could not grieve what she had never known. Her parents grieved the loss of their expectations for her but failed to see her remaining potential. Service providers would do well not to make the same mistake.

Disability and the Law

Justice for Tracy involves the recognition of equal rights for all Canadians regardless of dependency or limited physical and mental capabilities. No one should have to prove physical or mental competence before accessing legal, medical or other public services and rights. Eugenics has demonstrated the danger of such an approach. It begins with the Tracy Latimers but spreads to other vulnerable groups just as the Sue Rodriguez battle quickly spread to include Tracy.

Justice for Tracy must be the same as for any other victim. If she is treated differently, Canadian law can discriminate against any devalued people. The result would be a two-tiered justice system; this case clearly shows where disabled people would end up in such a system. The law does not and should not allow discrimination against any minority group, and disabled people are not an exception. And since anyone can become disabled, anything jeopardizing the rights of the Tracy Latimers has the potential to jeopardize the rights of any Canadian.

The Latimer case has generated a strong push for leniency in cases like this one. University of Manitoba law professor, Barney Sneiderman, has proposed a third degree of murder and admits that it would apply when the victim is disabled. Others, like a Winnipeg *Free Press* editorial, want minimum sentencing eliminated to allow judges leeway for what they call more appropriate sentencing in mercy killings. Still others want to completely legalize euthanasia as well as assisted suicide.

There is no middle ground on these issues. What passes for neutrality is really support for these changes. It is an attempt to dismiss some human lives without jeopardizing all. As Dick Sobsey has written, "Neutrality in the face of homicide is no moral high ground."[5]

The Charter says Canadians value equal rights for all citizens. If we pay only lip service to that, we lose the central principle of equality. Without equal rights we have no rights. Instead we have privileges for a few.

The Latimer case demonstrates how dangerous the proposed changes to the murder law would be. No safeguards can ever protect the many other disabled people like Tracy from the prevailing negative attitudes of those who know them only by their disabilities.

Lawyers, judges and police need more education on disability issues relating to the justice system. Laws protecting disabled citizens already exist but words on paper are not enough. These laws must also be enforced just as they are for other victims.

Quality of Life

This catch phrase has largely become a euphemism for negative perceptions about age, illness and disability.

In the Latimer case it has also been twisted to a new purpose. With Sue Rodriguez it described self-evaluation but with this case many presumed to judge the value of Tracy's life for her. Tracy's parents, her doctors and total strangers decided that, because of her inability to speak, they had the right to pronounce a helpless child's life meaningless and valueless. That is not justice for Tracy.

End-of-Life, Assisted Suicide and Euthanasia

This murder has repeatedly been sidetracked into discussions about assisted suicide or euthanasia and compared to cases bearing few similarities to this one. Merely placing Tracy alongside Sue Rodriguez created the impression that Tracy was terminally ill. This in turn lent credence to Robert Latimer's claim that he was helping her commit suicide.

The discussions did not investigate the validity of Latimer's assertions or show that Tracy's severe cerebral palsy did not in itself make her terminally ill. In light of the Canadian research showing that most such children live to the age of thirty or longer with the aid of good care and feeding tubes, it is probably more accurate to say that her lack of a feeding tube left her severely malnourished. However, although this case does not belong in discussions about end-of-life, the fact that it has been placed there proves how dangerous it would be to legalize euthanasia and assisted suicide.

It also proves how the negative bias confuses disability with terminal illness. That confusion substantiated by disabled people's experiences with general attitudes about disability confirms the danger in legalizing proposed end-of-life options. Unlimited personal freedom at the end of life can paradoxically end free choice. The right to choose an assisted death comes with the threat of getting it but not necessarily at one's own choosing.

Anne Mullens says in her book, *Timely Death*, that fewer than 5 percent of terminally ill people would choose an assisted death.[6] Dr. Harvey Max Chochinov, professor of psychiatry and the palliative care division of family medicine at the University of Manitoba, shows that the patients most likely to request an assisted death are those suffering from treatable clinical depression, those whose pain is under-treated and those whose support networks don't meet their needs.[7]

Chochinov writes that most physicians have only eight to ten hours of training in palliative care and symptom management and that "doctors who support legislation to support physician-hastened death ... are most likely to be physicians who have the least skill in managing end-of-life symptoms."

Proponents of assisted suicide and euthanasia would trust the judgement of doctors unskilled in pain management.

The decision on legalizing assisted suicide and/or euthanasia would be influenced by the pervasive and systematic bias toward disabled people. In the Latimer case and elsewhere misguided perceptions are leading to the conclusion that, for disabled people, compassion dictates "death with dignity" where for others it dictates life-prolonging medical intervention. Legalizing euthanasia would give free reign to such sentiments but leave disabled citizens powerless to defend themselves, even in court.

It is easy to see that with these options, factors other than compassion will inevitably creep into the decision-making process—economics, scapegoating or, as with Robert and Laura Latimer, fear, fatigue and misinformation.

Prof. Arthur Schafer, ethics professor and director of the Centre for Professional and Applied Ethics at the University of Manitoba, has already suggested economic benefits of do-not-resuscitate orders. In a November 14, 1998 article in the Winnipeg *Free Press* he wrote of the

Andrew Sawatzky case, "Keep in mind that one person's provision is another person's deprivation. The resources that are spent in a vain effort to deny our mortality are then not available to help those who can be genuinely helped: the sick, the vulnerable, the disabled, whose care ought to be our highest priority."[8]

Andrew Sawatzky, an older patient in a Winnipeg medical facility, Riverview Health Centre, has Parkinson's Disease and could have been described as sick, vulnerable, disabled. Yet Schafer did not want him included in these categories. Tracy Latimer was disabled, vulnerable and a lot younger than Sawatzky. She was not dying. She, too, could have benefited from the medical interventions she was denied. Yet Schafer has repeatedly and publicly supported Robert Latimer, not Tracy.

True rights hold in bad times as well as good. Equal rights must hold for everyone and guide all Canadians through thick and thin, regardless of cutbacks and other threats to services. The law as it stands protects equal rights for disabled citizens as well as everyone else. It should not be eroded just because people identify with Robert Latimer.

The Value of Human Life

To value only some lives is to choose a dangerous path. There is no consensus on the value of human life, on which life is worthless or when life loses its meaning. The eugenics program lasting in Alberta until the early 1970s showed that, once we devalue some life, we are on a slippery slope.

Similarly, within weeks of Sue Rodriguez losing her Supreme Court appeal, her cause, which focussed on autonomous choice, had come to include the killing of a defenceless child who had no choice in her own death. If the shift away from autonomy in establishing "quality of life" continues, then the new quality of life will inevitably be linked with the individual's worth as established by the community. From there it is not a great leap to other decisions also made in the name of communal good, even if it means sacrificing the interests of the individual. The Latimer case has demonstrated that, in the minds of some Canadians, this new standard is desirable when the victim is disabled.

Unless all human lives are respected equally, life is a privilege, not a right. If the rights of one group of citizens can be as easily eroded as they were in the Latimer case, then the same can happen to other marginalized people—poor, elderly, gay and lesbian and racialized minorities.

Ultimately, in dehumanizing others we dehumanize ourselves. If we refuse to see value in the lives of the unvalued, then we are the blind, not they. If we refuse to listen to the voices of the Tracy Latimers, then we are the deaf, not they. If we cannot accept the weakest among us, then we are weaker than they, for we then cannot accept our own weaknesses.

Disabled People in the Future

Disabled advocates are facing a major hurdle. Once again they must convince other Canadians that they have a right to the same services as everyone else, that they have a right to be here, that their lives are as valuable as anyone else's.

Tracy Latimer herself will never be heard and, as Dr. Chochinov wrote, "No one can presume to fully understand the circumstances or anguish of another human being."[9] The voice of disabled advocates who represent the majority of disabled people and are informed about disability issues are the closest Canadians can come to hearing Tracy. That voice is valid. It must be heard.

Notes

1. Michael D. Fitz-Jones, "Victims of the Latimer Case," p. 4.
2. Michael F. Giangreco (September 7, 1995). "The Stairs Don't Go Anywhere!"
3. Michael F. Giangreco (September 7, 1995). "The Stairs Don't Go Anywhere!"
4. Ellen J. Langer and Benzion Chanowitz, "Mindfulness/Mindlessness," p. 80.
5. Dick Sobsey, "The Media and Robert Latimer," p. 29.
6. Anne Mullens, *Timely Death*, p. 26.
7. Dr. Harvey Max Chochinov (October 24, 1998). "End-of-life care a test of society." Winnipeg *Free Press*, A15.
8. Arthur Schafer (November 14, 1998). "Who sets the limits on our health care?" Winnipeg *Free Press*, A4.
9. Dr. Harvey Max Chochinov (October 24, 1998). "End-of-life case a test of society." Winnipeg *Free Press*, A15.

Appendix

Below are Laura Latimer's entries in Tracy's communication books as recorded in the transcript of Robert Latimer's second trial in 1997. The notes are given in quotation marks.

The transcript of the second trial spelled Tracy's name differently than the first. It also misspelled "dessert" as "desert" so the notes below from pages 553 to 596 retain the transcript spellings.

1. October 8, 1992
   "Tracey was extra cheerful when she got home"
2. October 22, 1992
   "Tracey ate a good supper, and had meat and potatoes at bedtime, and I made a square.... That Tracey found very easy to eat, and she had about five little pieces, and she looked so happy.... She cried once early in the night, and I put her on her back, and she was fine the rest of the night"
3. October 29
   "Tracey is going to be a princess for Halloween"
4. November 1
   "Tracey is still cheerful, but has a very bad cold"
5. November 9
   "Tracey drank when she got home, she had a nap, and had a good supper. I think her hip was bothering her a lot. She had a B.M."
6. November 10
   "she slept a lot again today, ate all her lunch, starts to cough a lot when I give her a drink"
7. December 15
   "Tracey drank when she got home, then slept. She drank well at supper for her dad, but wouldn't eat well. When I got home she ate great and had pudding for desert. She had half a pudding at bedtime. Lindsay wrote a letter to Santa for Tracey. Do you have the purple and white top?"
8. January 4, 1993
   "Tracey had a drink when she got home, then a nap, ate a very good supper. She seems to enjoy picking the snowflakes off her

166

picture; I hope you don't mind, I let her."

9. January 11
   "Tracey drank when she got home, had a nap, B.M., had supper. At bedtime she had milk and meat and potatoes. She was a happy girl."

10. January 25
    "Tracey ate a very good supper, and was happy and alert all evening. I am sending her hair cut money. I wonder if you could quit putting perfume on Tracey, it really bothers me for some reason, must be allergic. I know it's probably part of her sensory stimulation program (Laura had written "problem" but corrected herself in court), maybe hand lotion would be better."

11. February 5
    "Tracey came home all smiles. Her cousins from Edmonton came to the farm Friday night, so that was fun."

12. February 8
    "Tracey came home very happy, had a drink and a little nap. When she got up she ate a very big supper. We had company for supper."

13. February 19
    "Tracey came home from the group home Friday night in a good mood. She has been eating and drinking just great. Had an Enercal (ph) at bedtime last night." (Enercal is a meal in a drink)

14. February 23
    "Tracey went to Saskatoon today for an appointment with Dr. Dzus. Tracey will be having surgery on her dislocated hip, but Dr. Dzus wants to give her back more chance to heal because it's not even a year since her back surgery. She has to see Dr. Dzus again in October, and surgery will likely be late in the fall. Tracey was glad to lay down when she got home, but she did fine all day. Please send Tracey to the group home after school Wednesday, and Thursday she can come home."

15. March 5
    "Tracey was a happy girl, ate and drank fine

16. March 15
    "Tracey was a very happy girl, ate and drank great, rocked with her dad for a long time."

17. March 31
    "Tracey was very cheerful. B.M. before supper."

18. April 3
    "Tracey was the worst girl at the sleep-over, up at ten to seven, laughing and vocalizing. She was really good the rest of the day. Lindsay read to her." (Lindsay's birthday was April 4)

19. April 11
    "Brian and Lindsay got up at 5:30 a.m. to hunt for eggs. We spent

most of Easter day at Tracey's cousin Lynn's place. Lynn is married to Reg Ross, who is Georgina Thomas's brother. There were lots of cousins and kids, and grandma and grandpa were there. Tracey spent a happy day, she ate a nice supper, and really enjoyed the deserts."

20. April 18

"Tracey was back to her old self the last few days, eating and drinking fine, but tonight at supper she brought up. She had two Opsite (ph) bandages on over the holidays, but, if anything, her sore looked worse. The last few days I've been letting air get at her sore as much as possible. I've got some callous bandages, so I hope that provides a cushion."

21. April 22

"Tracey seemed cheerful and more like her old self, ate great, had a bath."

22. April 2

"Tracey had a good weekend. Dirty diapers both days. She did cough up a little phlegm, but seemed happy and ate fine."

23. April 2

"Tracey had an early supper which she ate just fine, fruit for desert. She laid down. Janet Wallace came over while she was laying down. When I came home I gave Tracey a pudding. She was a happy girl."

24. May 5

"Janet Wallace got off the bus with Tracey. When I got home Tracey had spaghetti for supper, she ate it, but so slowly. I think she was wishing for more meat and potatoes. She loved the bells. I gave Brian heck, because I thought he was hitting his glass with a pen. We laughed when I realized it was Tracey and her bells."

25. May 6

"Tracey had a snooze when she got home, enjoyed her chicken supper, sat in her wheelchair after supper, happy girl."

26. May 10

"Tracey was happy. If she acts like her tooth hurts again let me know, because the dentist told me to watch for that with her discoloured tooth. She had milk and a baby food supper when she got home. Janet baby-sat her. When I got home from Brian's ball practice she had a real supper of meat and potatoes. She had a small B.M. I left her diaper open at bedtime to let air—to get air at her sore. Her leg seemed sore when she went to bed."

"Tracey cried during the night, around 12:30. When I went to see her she had soaked the bed. After I helped her she was happy."

27. May 12

"Tracey ate a very good ham supper, she was a very happy girl, drank well, glass and a half of milk at bedtime. I noticed there was still a pill in her pill bottle, so I'm not sure if she missed at lunch time, or if I sent extra. Anyway, she had her pill at summertime (supper time?), so she's fine. Sarah Stadnyck (ph) baby-sat Tracey and Lindsay for a while tonight. Brian has joined minor ball, so that's why Tracey has had so many baby-sitters lately."

28. May 13
"Sometimes I put Tracey's medicine in her bag at night, sometimes I do it in the morning, and I could easily have done it both times.... Lindsay painted Tracey's nails, Tracey chose red, as usual. She wore her splint, I think it is quite comfortable for her."

29. May 19
"Tracey's cousins, Jenny and Neil, and Aunt Dorothy from Edmonton were here shortly after four o'clock. After supper we had a bonfire and Tracey sat outside until about nine o'clock. It was a beautiful night. Tracey seemed especially alert and happy, she snoozed off and on during the meeting in the afternoon."

30. May 23
"I was so pleased Friday night when I looked at Tracey's pressure sore and it was all healed up.... Today Tracey stayed in bed until ten o'clock, then she had a huge breakfast, two soft boiled eggs and pancakes in the blender. Didn't eat a great lunch though. For supper we had a picnic at Finlayson Island, Wannell's picked us up in their motor home. Tracey went in her wheelchair, and we used tie downs to strap her in. She seemed tickled with the outing, ate a very good supper, especially enjoyed lemon pie for desert. She slept on the bed in the motor home on the way back, had milk and pudding at bedtime. "

31. May 27
"Tracey ate and drank fine, and was cheerful."

32. June 7
"Tracey was happy but did not eat her supper very well."

33. June 14
"Tracey ate a great supper, and was happy."

34. June 21
"Tracey had a good weekend, sat out on the deck lots. Grandma and grandpa came yesterday, she was so happy to see grandma. One bad thing, Tracey brought up her supper. I don't know why, she was eating great. I gave her another supper at bedtime."

At the end of June Tracy had her first trial respite stay at the group home in North Battleford and another shortly after. Then she spent three months there from July 5 to October 3. During these times there were no notes.

35. October 3

"Tracey came home late this afternoon, she got lots of attention. Tracey ate a great –"

36. October 4

"Tracey ate a good supper, and ate her desert before she went to bed. She seemed more comfortable. The green badges on Tracey's tray are what she won at bowling, she did the best in her class. Theresa (Huyghebaert) said Tracey threw up about three times over the three months."

37. October 6

"Tracey had a good evening, her hip seemed better at night than in the morning, she was quite cheerful."

38. October 13

"Tracey went to the group home for the weekend. Picked her up on Monday....B.M. Tuesday she went to Saskatoon, ate great." (Tuesday, October 12)

39. October 18

"Tracey kept everything down, so that was good. She was quite cheerful."

40. October 19

"Tracey was good, ate and drank fine." "Tracey was good, ate really well, had a bath, Bob bathed her."

The re-examination by defence counsel, Mark Brayford, about the communication books included the following entries in the communication books. He said he didn't want to go through the whole year, implying that he could.

1. October 13

"Tracey ate an early supper, but did not eat very well. She had a very sloppy, dirty diaper, had a nap. When she got up she drank a full can of Boost very easily. Later she had the rest of her supper. Had a bath. Tracey has a small sore at the base of her spine I want to keep an eye on, I want it open to the air as much as possible."

2. October 16

"Tracey ate an excellent supper so easily, but then when I laid her down she brought up. Later she drank a can of Boost."

3. October 17

"Tracey had a sloppy diaper early in the day yesterday. Last night she brought up before she went to bed. She cried a few times in the night and had to have her position changed.... She brought up her supper. She was only about halfway through and I wasn't pushing her at all. It is really discouraging. She had a bath."

Glossary of Disability Organizations Acronyms

ACCD: Alberta Committee of Citizens with Disabilities formed in 1972, originally the Alberta Committee of Action Groups for the Disabled, then the Alberta Committee of Consumer Groups of Disabled Persons, and the Alberta Committee of Disabled Citizens

BCCPD: British Columbia Coalition of People with Disabilities, formed in 1978.

CCD: Council of Canadians with Disabilities, formerly COPOH, the Coalition of Provincial Organizations of the Handicapped, founded in 1976.

COPHAN: Confederation des Organismes de Personnes Handicapees du Québec, formation date unknown.

COPOH: Coalition of Provincial Organizations of the Handicapped, now the Council of Canadians with Disabilities or CCD, founded in 1976.

CRCD: The Canadian Rehabilitation Council for the Disabled

DPI: Disabled Peoples' International, formed at its first World Congress in Singapore, 1981.

MLPD: Manitoba League of Persons with Disabilities formed in 1974, formerly the Society for Manitobans with Disabilities or MLPH.

NSLEO or LEO: Nova Scotia League for Equal Opportunities; founded in 1979.

PEICOD or COD: Prince Edward Island Council of the Disabled, founded in 1975.

PUSH: Persons United for Self-Help in Ontario, formed in 1981, now defunct.

RI: Rehabilitation International, formerly International Society for Crippled Children; founded in 1922.

SVPD usually called The Voice or The Saskatchewan Voice: Saskatchewan Voice of People with Disabilities, formed in 1973.

UHGO: United Handicapped Groups of Ontario, formation date unknown; stepped aside in 1981 for formation of PUSH

CNIB: Canadian National Institute for the Blind, an agency.

SMD: Society for Manitobans with Disabilities, formerly the Society for Crippled Children and Adults, an agency.

References

Alberta Committee of Action Groups of the Disabled. 1981. *The Disabled Consumer Movement in Alberta*. *Edmonton*: Alberta Committee of Action Groups of the Disabled.

Altick, Richard D. 1973. *Victorian People and Ideas: A Companion for the Modern Reader of Victorian Literature*. New York: Norton.

Coalition of Provincial Organizations of the Handicapped. 1986. *Annual Report*, Tenth Anniversary, Winnipeg: Coalition of Provincial Organizations of the Handicapped.

Council of Canadians with Disabilities. 1995a. *Policy Resolutions: Fundamental Human Rights*. Winnipeg: Minutes of the Council of Canadians with Disabilities. January 21–22.

_____. 1995b. *Policy Resolutions: Fundamental Human Rights*. Winnipeg: Minutes of the Council of Canadians with Disabilities. February 10–11.

_____. 1996. *Policy Resolutions: Fundamental Human Rights*. Winnipeg: Minutes of the Council of Canadians with Disabilities. June 8.

_____. 1996 to 1999. *CCD Latimer Watch*. Winnipeg: Council of Canadians with Disabilities.

_____. 1997. *CCD Orientation Manual*, Winnipeg: Council of Canadians with Disabilities.

Crichton, J.U., M. Mackinnon and C.P. White. 1995. "The Life-Expectancy of Persons with Cerebral Palsy," *Developmental Medicine and Child Neurology* 37.

DeJong, Gerben G. 1979. "Independent Living: From Social Movement to Analytic Paradigm." abstract. *Archives of Physical Medicine and Rehabilitation* 60.

Derksen, Jim. 1980. "The Disabled Consumer Movement: Policy Implications for Rehabilitation Service Provisions." Unpublished abstract. Winnipeg: Manitoba League of Persons with Disabilities.

Driedger, Diane. 1989. *The Last Civil Rights Movement, Disabled Peoples' International*. London, England: C. Hurst and Co.

Driedger, Diane. 1983. "Organizing for Change, A History of the Manitoba League of the Physically Handicapped." Unpublished essay for the course, A History of Western Canada: Winnipeg: Manitoba League of Persons with Disabilities.

Eaton v. *Brant County Board of Education*. 1997. Supreme Court of Canada, 1 Supreme Court Reports 241. Online at URL:http://www.sco.csc.gc.ca/services.htm.

Emanuel, Ezekiel J. MD, PhD. 1994. "The History of Euthanasia Debates in the

References

United States and Britain," *Annals of Internal Medicine* 121(10).

Englander, David. 1998. *Poverty and Poor Law Reform in Britain.* London and New York: Addison Wesley Longman.

Enns, Henry. 1981. "Canadian Society and Disabled People: Issues for Discussion." *Canada's Mental Health* December 29(4).

Federal/Provincial/Territorial Ministers Responsible for Social Services. 1998. "In Unison: A Canadian Approach to Disability Issues." Unpublished Discussion Paper.

Fitz-James, Michael D. 1998. "Victims of the Latimer Case." *Canadian Lawyer* September.

Fraser, Derek. 1976. *The New Poor Law in the Nineteenth Century.* New York: St. Martin's Press.

Giangreco, Michael F. 1995. "The Stairs Don't Go Anywhere!" *Physical Disabilities: Education and Related Services.* September 7. Online at http://www.normemma.com/arstairs.htm.

Gilroy, Goss Inc., Management Consultants. 1995. "Interdepartmental Evaluation of the National Strategy for the Integration of Persons with Disabilities." Unpublished report.

Hilton, Boyd. 1988. *The Age of Atonement,* Oxford: Clarendon Press.

Ingstad, Benedicte and Susan Reynolds (eds.). 1995. *Disability and Culture.* Berkeley: University of California Press.

Katz, Irwin et al. 1988. "Attitudinal Ambivalence and Behavior Toward People with Disabilities." In Harold Yuker (ed.), *Attitudes Toward Persons with Disabilities.* New York: Springer Publishing Co.

Langer, Ellen J. and Benzion Chanowitz. 1988. "Mindfulness/Mindlessness: A New Perspective for the Study of Disability." In Harold Yuker (ed.), *Attitudes Toward Persons with Disabilities.* New York: Springer Publishing Co.

Lowy, Frederick H., Douglas M. Sawyer and John R. Williams. 1993. "Lessons From Experience." *Canadian Physicians and Euthanasia.* Toronto: Canadian Medical Association.

MacEachen, Sara Ellen. 1993. *Persons United for Self-Help in Ontario.* Toronto: Persons United for Self-Help in Ontario.

McLaren, Angus. 1998. *Our Own Master Race: Eugenics in Canada 1885 to 1945.* Oxford University Press.

Mullens, Anne. 1997. *Timely Death.* Toronto: Vintage Press.

Oliver, Michael and Priscilla Anderson. 1998. "Theories of disability in health practice and research." *British Medical Journal* November 21. 317(7170).

Pringle, Heather. June 1997. "Alberta Barren." *Saturday Night.*

R. v. *Robert W. Latimer.* 1994. The Court of Queen's Bench for Saskatchewan, Judicial Centre of Battleford, QB CR. #37 of AD 1994.

R. v. *Robert W. Latimer.* 1997. The Court of Queen's Bench for Saskatchewan, Judicial Centre of Battleford, Q.B.J. #37 of AD 1994.

Scott, Robert A. 1991. *The Making of Blind Men: A Study of Adult Socialization.* New Jersey, Rutgers University: Transaction Publications.

Self-Counsel Press. 1995. *Living Will, Form.* Vancouver: Self-Counsel Press.

Simpson, Allan J. 1980. "Consumer Groups: Their Organization and Function." Unpublished report to the World Congress on Rehabilitation International.

Winnipeg: Manitoba League of Persons with Disabilities.

Smith, Wesley J. 1997. *Forced Exit: The Slippery Slope from Assisted Suicide to Legalized Murder.* New York: Random House - Times Books.

Sobsey, Dick. 1998. "The Media and Robert Latimer." In *The Latimer Case: Reflections of People with Disabilities.* Winnipeg: Council of Canadians with Disabilities.

Somerville, Margaret A. 1997. "Euthanasia by Confusion." *UNSW Law Journal.*

Statistics Canada. 1991. "Health and Activity Limitation Survey." *Adults with Disabilities: Their Employment and Education Characteristics.* (Cat. No. 82-554.) Ottawa: Statistics Canada.

Stewart, Brian. 1998. "A Parental Perspective." In *The Latimer Case: The Reflections of People with Disabilities.* Winnipeg: Council of Canadians with Disabilities.

Stienstra, Deborah and Patrick Kellerman. 1999. "Taking action on the United Nations Standard Rules on Disability." Unpublished report. Winnipeg: University of Winnipeg.

Weinberg, Nancy. 1988. "Another Perspective: Attitudes of People with Disabilities." In Harold Yuker (ed.), *Attitudes Toward Persons with Disabilities.* New York: Springer Publishing Co.

Wright, Beatrice A. 1988. "Attitudes and the Fundamental Negative Bias." In Harold Yuker (ed.), *Attitudes Toward Persons with Disabilities.* New York: Springer Publishing Co.

Interviews

Arnold, Ed. November 23, 1998. Telephone interview.

Beachell, Laurie. May 19, 1998. Personal interview.

Brodsky, Greg. March 11, 1999.Telephone interview.

Danforth, Pat. June 26, 1998. Telephone interview.

Derksen, Jim. July 6, 1998. Telephone interview.

Ducharme, Theresa. June 22, 1998. Personal interview.

Graham, Mel. May 19, 1998, May 27, 1998. Personal interviews. March 30, 1999. Telephone interview.

Heselton, Georgina. June 20, 1998. Telephone interview.

Lambeth, Catherine Anne "Cal". February 8, 1999. Personal interview.

Martin, David. November 30, 1998. Personal interview.

Mitchell QC, Grant. January 8, 1999. Telephone interview.

Norman, Eric. June 6, 1998. Personal interview.

Penner, Cateland. January 11, 1999. Personal interview.

Preston, Dr. Allan. June 30, 1998. Telephone interview.

Richards, Bob. August 3, 1999. Telephone interview

Rosner, Mike. November 25, 1998. Personal interview.

Rowan, Dr. Vivienne. October 15, 1998. Telephone interview.

Schnellert, Laura. January 11, 1999. Personal interview.

Simpson, Allan. November 14, 1998. Personal interview.

Simpson, Clare. May 29, 1998. Telephone interview. November 10, 1998. Personal interview.

Simpson, Julie. November 14, 1998. Personal interview.

Sisco, Pat. December 3, 1998. Personal interview.

Stewart, Brian and Anne and children: Nicolas (Nick) Stewart, Eva Marie Stewart, Noah, Ericka Stewart, Jonathon (Jon) Stewart, Harley. November 15, 1998. Personal group interview.

Strang, Dr. Vicki. March 20, 1999. Telephone interview.

Winnipeg Humane Society. June 30, 1998. Telephone interview.

About the Author

Ruth Enns grew up in a farming village in Manitoba. As the middle child of a farm couple who raised primarily grain, she is well acquainted with Canadian rural prairie life.

She got her B.A. and B.Ed. from the University of Manitoba and spent eight years teaching in rural schools. Shortly after her marriage in 1981, illness forced her out of the profession so she turned to freelance writing after studying Creative Communications at Red River Community College.

Ms. Enns acquired a sensitivity to the Canadian disability rights movement through her own experiences with disability resulting from polio and glaucoma. She was also briefly involved in the early development of the Manitoba League of the Physically Handicapped, now the Manitoba League of Persons with Disabilities although since the seventies she has not been involved with any of these organizations.

Since 1983 she and her husband have lived in rural Manitoba.

Electronic versions of this book, in HTML, as well as a limited number of large print photocopies are available to individuals from:
Fernwood Publishing
Box 9409, Stn. A,
Halifax, Nova Scotia,
B3K 5S3
Tel: (902) 422-3302
Fax: (902) 422-3179
fernwood@istar.ca
www.home.istar.ca/~fernwood